THE
ROAD TRIP
SURVIVAL
GUIDE

TIPS *and* TRICKS *for* PLANNING ROUTES,
PACKING UP, *and* PREPARING
for ANY UNEXPECTED ENCOUNTER
ALONG *the* WAY

THE ROAD TRIP

SURVIVAL GUIDE

TIPS *and* TRICKS *for* PLANNING ROUTES,
PACKING UP, *and* PREPARING
for ANY UNEXPECTED ENCOUNTER
ALONG *the* WAY

ROB TAYLOR

TILLER PRESS

New York   London   Toronto   Sydney   New Delhi

An Imprint of Simon & Schuster, Inc.
1230 Avenue of the Americas
New York, NY 10020

First Tiller Press paperback edition May 2021

TILLER PRESS and colophon are trademarks of Simon & Schuster, Inc.

For information about special discounts for bulk purchases, please contact Simon & Schuster Special Sales at 1-866-506-1949 or business@simonandschuster.com.

The Simon & Schuster Speakers Bureau can bring authors to your live event. For more information or to book an event, contact the Simon & Schuster Speakers Bureau at 1-866-248-3049 or visit our website at www.simonspeakers.com.

Interior design by Jennifer Chung

Illustrations by Peter Donnelly
Directions icon by Andrejs Kirma/The Noun Project
Compass icon by Dmitry Baranovskiy/The Noun Project
Turn right, turn left, road, right, traffic sign, and
two way icons by HideMaru/The Noun Project

Manufactured in the United States of America

1   3   5   7   9   10   8   6   4   2

Library of Congress Cataloging-in-Publication Data has been applied for.

ISBN 978-1-9821-7706-5
ISBN 978-1-9821-7707-2 (ebook)

CONTENTS

FOREWORD

I'VE BEEN LUCKY enough to have had a career in travel for more than twenty-two years. Most of my travel takes place on planes that get me to far-flung destinations in the quickest manner possible, and yet even with the efficiency of aircraft, my favorite way to travel has been and will always be the road trip.

When I was growing up in the 1970s and '80s, getting on a plane wasn't even a consideration; the road trip was family travel. Driving for ten hours just meant packing up the station wagon and leaving at 4:00 a.m. instead of 9:00, still in our PJs and ready to fight with the family dog like it was another annoying sibling. I still remember the pajamas I wore, the cooler full of bologna sandwiches, and the lack of seat belts.

I highly doubt my parents gave too much thought to the importance the memories of these road trips would have in my life. How could they? They were parents before the word "parenting" was a thing. But now that I'm in full parent mode, road trips aren't just a way to get to a destination—they're what happens in between: the anticipation, the joy, the crankiness, the unexpected stops for slices of "famous" pie or even a half-decent restroom to put an end to the crankiness.

Reading this book will not only give you the best possible advice on how to plan a great family, solo, or romantic (I'd forgotten there was such a thing) road trip but also encourage a mindset that understands how all the planning is ultimately what allows you to enjoy the unexpected, to leave room for that thing you didn't know would become the highlight of your trip.

So call shotgun and pass me a bologna sandwich; I'm letting Rob be the driver. He knows the way.

—Samantha Brown

INTRODUCTION

EMBARKING ON ROAD trips has been an important part of American culture for nearly a century. Of course, it has evolved, and now more than ever it's become an important way to travel. I grew up going on road trips because that was the affordable way to take a vacation. As the years have gone by, just as with anything else, road trips have become more expensive. That said, they are still one of the best options for budget family travel, couple travel, or solo travel.

I remember being a kid and thinking that road trips were so much fun but at the same time equally as boring. Maybe it's because we did so many of them that I didn't appreciate them fully, or maybe because back then it was harder to entertain children for extensive periods of time, but now that I'm a dad, I've worked hard to make sure that the many trips we go on with our two kids are always fun and captivating.

As we go through the road trip survival guide, we'll tackle all kinds of topics including planning the most fun itineraries, making the actual car ride enjoyable for everyone, and discussing important ways to keep safety in mind as you journey down unknown roads.

The tips and suggestions in this book are coming to you from a place of experience and sometimes exasperation. What works for my family might not work for yours, and what works for my kids might actually be great advice to apply to a cranky spouse in the car. You decide what to do with all of this information.

As with any good advice, take it with a grain of salt. What I've learned on long drives through the mountains of California doesn't necessarily apply to beach hopping in Florida. And learning the hard way about snowmobile routes in Canada doesn't carry the same lesson as getting stuck on a back road in Mexico.

Ultimately, I want everyone to explore at their own speed and create new experiences and memories along the way. As you dig into the itineraries, know that these are suggestions and you've got the power to adjust the plans to best suit you and your travel buddies.

CHAPTER I

PLANNING

RESEARCHING DESTINATIONS AND ATTRACTIONS

A road trip can be anything from exploring locally or traveling three thousand miles from point A to point B. But what you do in between the points is what makes for exciting travel opportunities. I think it's important to start by considering the value of worthwhile sites and attractions. Endless highways and interstates serve the purpose of making travel time fly by. It's the interesting things off road that really make a road trip worthwhile.

BEST WEBSITES TO DISCOVER ROADSIDE ATTRACTIONS AND SIGHTS

In addition to being a published author, I run a travel blog. And that means that I'm always sharing what I find as I journey around with my family, usually in the moment on the blog or via social media. That also means I'm a big supporter of using other writers' travel blogs for research. There are many wonderful books that have been written over the years detailing sights and roadside attractions, but not all publications are maintained regularly and updated with current information. Websites are refreshed quite frequently, so the information on blogs and destination sites is very reliable.

The Value of Travel Blogs for Research

Once you know you're going on a road trip, set some time aside dedicated to reading recently updated travel blogs and destination websites. Not only does spending time on blog sites help you get a good understanding of the road ahead but you're also helping to support small businesses (yes, writers and bloggers are their own small businesses).

In running a travel blog, I've found that most of my experiences and writing come from being invited to visit new destinations. After spending time exploring, I then share what I've discovered as worthwhile recommendations. There's something to be said for the candid nature of independently run websites, and that's why I strongly recommend digging into travel blogs to find the most interesting sights.

Destination Brand Websites for Current Information

Destination websites are also invaluable. If you're going to be driving somewhere and want to enjoy local culture, checking out that local destination's website should give you accurate information about festivals and if anything is currently closed or out of operation.

A great example of this would be when events that are typically annual have been canceled due to a pandemic or recent weather events, such as a hurricane.

If you're digging through a destination website trying to curate your ideal trip, be aware that some towns' or regions' travel associations are membership-based versus being funded by tax dollars. What does this mean for you as a visitor?

Well, when you're reading up on the latest things to do via the Chamber of Commerce website, you're looking at information and activities provided by dues-paying members, or even people who have purchased a front-page space. This means they have the money to get in front of your eyes, but this might not always be the best choice.

Note: I would say that the majority of attractions and businesses that are a part of Chambers of Commerce are still small businesses, which we always encourage supporting. There are also larger attractions with outside funding (think about franchised restaurants or activities) that participate. Just always think about where your money is going as you plan your trips.

Another type of destination website you'll find is one that's run by the visitors' bureau or tourism board. Funded by taxes, they share all kinds of businesses in their community. You'll find a much broader collection of attractions, restaurants, and lodging options through a site like this.

SOCIAL MEDIA FOR TRIP PLANNING

As unreliable as it sounds, social media is also a great place to do research before a road trip. Browsing through hashtags on Instagram or Twitter will provide you with all kinds of posts from people who have recently traveled through where you're planning to visit. More than once, we've changed our plans on the fly after poking around on social media; we discovered either better options nearby or found out that the hiking trail we planned to climb was closed.

Social media was also a resource in finding out which roadside attractions were open when we did a cross-country relocation during the height of the coronavirus pandemic.

As irritating as social media can be, it can also be a boundless tool for research. And on that same note, contributing your own experiences and opinions to social media will help others who are also doing research. If you want to contribute to the online global travel community, share your road trip experiences honestly and using the appropriate social media tags.

Gatekeeping in Travel-Related Social Media

A common topic, both in social media and now in major magazine and news publications, is gatekeeping. *Gatekeeping* is defined as the act of controlling, and often limiting access to something intentionally.[1]

How does this apply to travel and social media research? It's quite simple, and you may or may not have been unknowingly exposed to this in the past.

What this means when you're researching travel via social media is that you may find a place, a gorgeous, calm, perfect pond with a magical waterfall cascading into it . . . and it's tagged as "Planet Earth" or "Keep nature wild" or a variety of different statements. Usually, the caption or proclamation in the post includes a statement telling the reader not to share the location of this perfect pond in order to preserve it.

The problem with this kind of gatekeeping is that the individuals sharing their travels on social media while also not sharing the location for the above reason are outwardly deciding that they were worthy of the experience but others are not. They're assuming others won't respect or appreciate the site the way they do.

As you venture out onto the road and share your experiences and discoveries, don't be a gatekeeper. Share where you are and how you left no trace. Encourage others to be aware and respectful, but don't try to bar them from sharing in the special spot you've found.

RESEARCHING EPIC VIEWS

Have you ever poked through a coffee-table book and seen epic views that you just can't even comprehend hiking to? I do this all the time and with a little research, I can often either find the exact same view or something comparable.

So how do you find amazing views when their exact map coordinates aren't available? It's simpler than you might realize.

Say you're flipping through some pages and see a beautiful picture of a canyon that you MUST see with your own eyes. Within the publication, look at the photo credit, and if the precise location isn't included, hop on the internet and search for the photographer who's credited and the approximate location. From here, you may either find a website by the actual photographer or a blog post detailing incredible views in that same area.

Another way to research beautiful places or hidden attractions is to, again, jump online, but this time look into an online map with user integrations and browse through pictures within the map layers. Here's an exercise to practice:

1. Choose a general location on an online map
2. Click onto a park, point of interest, or photo symbol
3. Look through user photos, many may have captions and information
4. Drill down even further in the map and you'll find photos users have uploaded at more pinpointed spots

This process works with many types of online maps, including maps within social media platforms.

As you learn new techniques for online research, road trip planning gets even more exciting. You'll find so many new, and often overlooked, points of interest to add to your itinerary.

DECIDING HOW FAR TO GO OFF COURSE

Whenever I build a road trip plan, I always make sure to add extra time in, either to each day or to the full calendar of the trip (more on this in the next section). The purpose of a time buffer is so that you can stay on schedule but also lean into the random dirt road you're curious about, or the completely unexpected public art park you just *have to* stop at.

As you start to plan your road trip itinerary, take into consideration how well you know the history or culture of where you're traveling to. Basic research might uncover that your path is actually a historic route full of small museums or iconic pie shops.

Both in planning and when we're actually on the road, our family follows this simple set of qualifiers before going off course. If we can score 3 out of 5, then it's worth the stop:

	A	B	
HAVE WE BEEN TO OR SEEN SOMETHING VERY SIMILAR BEFORE?	N	Y	
IS THERE A WOW-FACTOR OR TRUE CURIOSITY ABOUT IT?	Y	N	
DOES GOING OFF COURSE CHANGE WHERE WE SPEND THE NIGHT?	N	Y	
DO AT LEAST 50 PERCENT OF US HAVE AN INTEREST?	Y	N	
COULD THE WEATHER PREVENT US FROM ENJOYING IT WHEN WE ARRIVE?	N	Y	
IF COLUMN A IS MORE, THEN DO IT! TOTALS			

By nature, road trip travel needs to be a flexible experience. Uncertain road conditions or unforeseen traffic can have a big impact on how the drive actually goes. Enjoying a stop more than you expected, thus lingering longer, can throw a hiccup into how well you're making time.

It's okay to go off course a bit, either metaphorically or in reality, but have a backup plan in case you've derailed your trip a bit too much.

ROAD TRIP CALENDARING

Doesn't *calendaring* sound like such a corporate word? I mean, it is, but it very much applies to designing a road trip plan and successfully enjoying yourself to the max as well. When I talk about calendaring, I don't mean planning everything down to the minute for a trip. Instead, it's more about understanding and establishing important times and dates.

Getting to take a vacation and enjoying the process of traveling is such a treat. You could try to rush it all and cram everything in, or you can budget your time so that you aren't returning to real life even more burned out than when you left. You just have to be smart about calendaring!

ADDING A ROAD TRIP
TO YOUR LIFE CALENDAR

Some days I open my calendar on my laptop and just stare at the empty run of days. I think about how easy it would be to block out four . . . wait, seven . . . or maybe ten days.

Calendaring a road trip is more than just seeing available days off and filling them up. When I start a road trip plan, I always first consider my starting point.

- Do I need to plan for a day of travel, such as a flight, before I'm even on the road?
- Am I leaving from my own driveway during rush hour?

When you're determining your daily driving route, be sure you take into consideration the first day or pre-trip. To maximize our available time off, we often leave for road trips in the afternoon (hopefully before traffic sets in), so the end of our first day is usually about four hours from home. Of course, the destination is ultimately going to determine if that's an option for you, but if you can start traveling a half day earlier, you'll have more time to enjoy the sights once you're moving.

So, you know you're going on a trip. You know you can have a few hours of travel time on that last working day before you're slated to be on vacation (ideally). You know you need to be back at work on Day X. Now you can make your plan.

Note: If you're like me, I require being home for a full day to unpack and unwind before I can return to work—*and I work at home as my own boss!* If you need that cushion to get your work brain ready again, be sure to plan that when you're calendaring your road trip.

Flying to Drive: Traveling to the Beginning of Your Route

I used to think road trips could only start at home, and that we could only use our own vehicle, and then one day we decided that we could fly and then travel by car—and that too is a road trip! This change of viewpoint really opened doors for how we travel and the diversity of experiences we are able to enjoy.

The most scenic drives in North America don't usually start just outside the airport, but you'd be surprised what you can find very near where you land. When you're considering road trip ideas, be open to a flight to get to a different region if the budget allows. For example, an airport like Portland, Oregon (PDX), has the Columbia River Gorge National Scenic Area just to the east, so it's an easy addition if you're planning a trip heading west to the coast.

For example, our family was able to complete one of the best road trips in the USA by hopping on a plane from Seattle, Washington, to Bozeman, Montana. This short flight was inexpensive and gave us more than three extra days to enjoy exploring Montana and Wyoming.

Another time we flew into Fort Lauderdale for our first trip to the Florida Gulf Coast and picked up a campervan so we could enjoy a camping-style road trip without having to travel with our own equipment. Many more options are available when you allow yourself to fly to a road trip route starting point.

The point of all this: Don't limit your road trip vacation to just what's beyond your driveway. Pick someplace exotic and make it into a road trip. You can cut the total travel time to that incredible new place by hopping a plane first.

Road Trips: Leaving from Home

There's a lot to be said for being able to pack up for a road trip from your own home. For most families, this is by far the most economical option since you don't need to pay for flights or a rental car. This is also an opportunity to go beyond your backyard but not waste a day sitting in an airport.

Having grown up in the Seattle area, I'm very familiar with Washington State, so hopping in the car and just traveling within our own borders has always been easy and comfortable.

Venturing beyond our standards of Washington Wine Country or the Columbia River Gorge, we have gotten to visit places we had never considered in the past, including Idaho and rural Oregon. Wow! Inspired by a coffee-table book, our first trip through the Sawtooth Mountains was remarkable and was a destination that was never on our radar until we flipped through that book.

Deciding to stay closer to home does cut back on the amount of drive time to what you might consider your starting point (the first cool spot you stop, maybe). If exploring your home region allows you more time to relax versus covering a lot of ground, do it! Road tripping is all about creating a vacation that's right for you or your family.

How Much Time to Take Off for a Road Trip

Ooh, this is such a loaded topic. How much time should you take off for a road trip? Well, that depends on what you want to tackle. There are a few things to consider before dedicating yourself to taking a set amount of time off work.

First off, how long do you WANT to be on the road, not working? And how long CAN you be gone from work? Do you have paid time off (PTO) that you get to use to supplement your income?

Also, do you have pets? How long can they stay with friends or have a house sitter with them? Are you bringing a pet with you? Access to paid or approved time off from a job is one thing but settling on how long you can be away from a pet is another. Try using this quick tool to see how much time you *can* be away:

	EXAMPLE
AVAILABLE PTO:	15
DAYS OKAY TO BE AWAY FROM PET:	7
DAYS WITH A SECURED PET SITTER:	5
YOU CAN BE AWAY FOR WHICHEVER NUMBER OF DAYS IS LEAST	

There are so many variables, but here's how I like to plan out a good calendar request (see table). Also, knowing how my family travels and maintains interest or energy levels, I usually plan just one big sightseeing experience or hike per day, filling in the extra time with either relaxation or random discoveries.

By using the method of one big thing each day, our schedule provides plenty of room for error or allows for us to get distracted exploring beyond our predetermined itinerary. Half the fun comes from the unexpected dirt roads and random pit stops.

The following form can be used to decide how many days to take off from work or school, assuming a five-day workweek. If you can line up time off with weekend days, you'll see your vacation length grow substantially.

DESTINATION:	HOW MANY	MINIMUM ALLOWABLE
FULL TRAVEL DAYS		
BIG SIGHTSEEING / HIKING - 1 PER DAY		
ONLY RELAXATION / NO TRAVEL		
RECOVERY / BUFFER DAYS		
	IDEAL	MINIMUM REQUEST (SUBTRACT WEEKEND DAYS):

This is what the form looks like filled in when I'm actually planning a real trip for our family and taking into consideration limited time away from school or work:

DESTINATION: FLORIDA KEYS	HOW MANY	MINIMUM ALLOWABLE
FULL TRAVEL DAYS	2	2
BIG SIGHTSEEING / HIKING – 1 PER DAY	4	3
ONLY RELAXATION / NO TRAVEL	2	1
RECOVERY / BUFFER DAYS	1	0
	IDEAL	MINIMUM REQUEST (SUBTRACT WEEKEND DAYS): 4 DAYS OFF

Do you see how I would really love to have an eight- or nine-day trip but could only swing it by requesting four days off? Sometimes we make grand plans that would take a ton of time, but reality sets in and we may have to be okay with more mild adventures.

Flexibility is key when planning a road trip and securing the necessary time in your calendar.

Tip: Do you have a job where you work remotely or are your kids in virtual school? If so, you may be able to really extend your time away if you can add a few working or school days into the mix. Finding a nice vacation rental or hotel with reliable internet service will allow a great deal of flexibility in your calendar.

Planning Travel Around Holiday Weekends

At first thought, planning a road trip or short getaway on a holiday weekend sounds like a great idea and a way to take advantage of having an extra day off from work or school. Yes, you do get more time, but you also get more people (because they had the same thought you did).

While not every destination or road trip itinerary is going to be heavily impacted by holiday traffic, the more popular spots near metropolitan areas will for sure see many more visitors. Holiday weekends are both a blessing and a curse.

So, how do you take advantage of a holiday weekend without feeling the full impact of crowds? Easy.

Most travelers are hitting the road early on the afternoon of the last working day before a holiday weekend. What if you left a day or two before everyone else? And a lot of people are returning home on the last day of the holiday break, so what if you extended your trip by a day? If your time off or work calendar would allow, changing your start or end date can really have a positive impact on the travel experience, and there may be smaller crowds at your destination.

And when it comes to enjoying the destination during a more crowded holiday weekend, by leaving a day earlier or staying an additional day, you'll have access to more popular sights while everyone else is heading home.

On the busy days when there are extra travelers out and about, those are great days to focus on relaxation or activities earlier in the day. If you arrived early and aren't feeling the drag of a long day of travel while everyone else is, you can beat the crowds to whatever fun you have planned.

Tales from the Road: Forgetting the Return Trip

I wish I could say that I haven't learned many lessons from traveling, but I have. And this lesson I've had to relearn.

On two separate occasions I've done road trips to Southern California from Washington. These were both well-planned trips, including hotel reservations, Disneyland, and more. On both trips we had an amazing time but didn't realize that we didn't plan correctly for the return drive, which takes either two days or one *extremely long* day.

Realizing on Saturday that your return drive the next day would be nineteen hours means a lot of stress and a tired crew. For our own safety, because a nineteen-hour drive is too much for one day, we left midway through Saturday, found a hotel when we got tired, and finished the drive the next day.

The second time I made this error we realized it sooner. We were in Los Angeles and had big plans for the day, but around 9:00 a.m. it hit me that the drive back north was a two-day drive, just like it was the previous time this happened. We were able to adjust plans a whole day earlier than the first time, but seriously, calendaring a trip really isn't that hard.

I just chalk these experiences up to being in my twenties and caring more about enjoying every possible moment than being logical.

PS: I haven't made this mistake since 2008. Hooray for growing and learning!

PLANNING A DAILY SCHEDULE

Know your limits. That's it. That's the section.

Of course, there's more to it than that, but understanding your limits and everyone's energy level is extremely important. I was the king of thinking we could do everything in one day. It would take getting on location before I would actually start paring down our daily itinerary.

Here's how I do things now, and five years of using this method has taken our family trip from fast-moving and fun to memorable and meaningful. I'm using a portion of a trip plan for illustration purposes.

- Step 1: Make a list of the big activities along your route

- Step 2: Order activities by where they fall on your route
- Step 3: Assign days for your activities and note how long things may take

Note: If you do the math on the schedule example, you'll see that the actual time noted doesn't match up with the time stamps. That's because there's a bit of a buffer built into each activity. One of the joys of travel is surprising yourself with how much you *can* enjoy everything. Don't rush yourself.

As you plan out your days, if you're doing a down-and-back, meaning you're following the same route home, you can always add points of interest that you missed on the first leg to your return trip.

Remember, every road trip is different and there's no single correct way to plan your time. Err on the side of free time so you can fill it when you discover activities or places that you truly enjoy and didn't expect.

Allowing for Unplanned Stops and Sights

So, you've made your loose plan for your road trip and now you're ready to hit the road. You're on your way to someplace new and you've got your sights set on your first big stop. You see a hand-painted sign on the side of the highway: "BEST HOMEMADE PIES IN ALL OF KLICKITAT COUNTY . . ."

What do you do? Do you jump at the chance to see if the sign maker is a liar or do you keep going? I think that depends on your personality type.

→ The Schedule Buffer

If you've built your daily schedule or overall itinerary with buffer time, you have afforded yourself the opportunity to get distracted by the small things you couldn't have planned for. Like the best pies in the county.

Buffer time is going to look different for everyone. For me, making a daily schedule with overestimated time for driving and activities ensures we can take advantage of lots of unplanned stops.

→ The Home Base Explorer

I've done trips with other people where I've let them do the planning and have seen that other travel personalities create very different schedules. My primary observation of others' methods is that some prefer to get to a destination and then explore versus exploring along the way.

If you're a home base explorer, that's fine. A great way to allow for unplanned stops and activities when you like to GET TO your destination instead of stopping along the way is to build unstructured time into your plan. This can be a whole day with a list of ideas or a chunk of a day with no plan.

When we travel with friends, we use blocks like this for splitting up to do different activities, either mixing families or giving us all a sometimes much-needed break from each other.

If you're going to build your road trip days with free time around a home base, be sure that you've still done at least minimal research to have a jumping-off point. Oh, and don't underestimate the value of just using that time to relax.

MAKING A ROAD TRIP GREEN

Road trips traditionally have been considered a great budget option for traveling, but did you know they are also a low-impact type of travel? It's true! The carbon footprint of a family of four driving is far less than four people flying. More on that in a moment.

Keeping sustainability in mind with travel has become paramount to ensuring the next generation is able to experience the world as we have, or better. Considering climate change, cultural pillaging, and plastic pollutants, there are many ways travelers, particularly families, can make small changes for a maximum impact. And that starts by road tripping.

MINIMIZING YOUR CARBON FOOTPRINT IN TRAVEL

Nobody likes to talk about the amount of pollution travel generates, from the carbon emissions of airplanes to gray water from cruise ships. Researching your transportation or tour company before booking a trip is the first step to minimizing your own carbon footprint.

Things to look for when booking travel:

- Transparency from the company re: waste disposal and exceeding regulations
- Corporate Social Responsibility report, which should include information about how the company is offsetting its carbon footprint
- Chances to book bicycles instead of cars
- Curated eco-tours that vet and plan green transport and activities

Things to avoid:

- Peak dates/times for travel
- Mass transport through pristine areas
- Flying when rail service is available
- Layovers—the greatest pollution occurs during takeoff, so book direct flights

When you look at the carbon footprint of a road trip versus flying, it's actually quite impressive to see how much less impact a driving vacation has than a flight.

In 2019 the BBC released the following data around carbon emissions and other pollutants based on the mode of transportation (numbers have been converted from the metric system):[2]

	POLLUTANTS PER TRIP IN POUNDS
500-MILE DOMESTIC FLIGHT- 1 PERSON	450
500-MILE DOMESTIC FLIGHT- 4 PEOPLE	1,799
500-MILE DRIVE- 1 PERSON	303
500-MILE DRIVE- 4 PEOPLE	305

When I'm planning travel for my family, I always try to keep in mind how much better for the environment and local economies a road trip is than flying to our final destination.

PRESERVING UNIQUE COMMUNITIES AND NATURE

As I write this, my kids are playing in the other room. Someday, they'll be out traveling on their own. I can't help but wonder if they'll get to experience the same pockets of wonder around the world that we have. I wonder if the small towns in Montana or pueblos in New Mexico will be the same for their families as they were for our visits.

Historic Communities vs. Tourism

With the rise of self-managed room and accommodation rentals, such as Airbnb and Booking.com, apartments and cabins with "rustic charm" and "seaside cottages" are becoming accessible to tourists. While this is an attractive type of lodging and will no doubt create lasting memories, the growth and expansion of these is wedging out the locals in many communities. The profit of renting out rooms or whole houses to tourists is greater than providing housing to the local population.

"Why should I *not* book a quaint cottage in wine country for a week if it's putting money back into the community?" You're correct, much of the money brought into these small towns by lodging dollars stays in the same place and helps, but in the meantime those who don't have a piece of the pie are forced to the margins of their hometown. The people who work in the destinations and give them their charm and hospitality are increasingly unable to live in the community where they and their families work.

→ What You Can Do Instead

Putting money back into the community you're visiting is very important. So how do you do that without booking the private accommodations mentioned? Simple.

Wherever you go there are small inns, boutique lodging, B&Bs . . . These types of accommodations are typically locally owned and operated, employing locals and keeping the tourism dollars directly in the community. In many cases, the rooms are similarly priced and equally charming.

You can still plan a wonderful stay in a quaint town, but you're helping to preserve the way of life *and* helping to build up the economy.

Improper Wildlife Tourism

Another growing issue with travel, both in exotic destinations and on popular road trip routes, is wildlife tourism. While the tides have shifted from sport hunting to now just observing wildlife, there is still a tremendous impact on endemic populations.

America's national parks have seen an influx of visitors in recent years, exponentially greater than previous decades. The bays and straits of tropical destinations have more and more tours operating now that encourage swimming with dolphins and whale sharks in the wild and observing sea turtles in their natural habitat.

"Why is this impacting wildlife when it's just observing?" Ideally, observation would have no impact, but the droves of people putting added weight on the ecosystem of a contained area is unfathomable. The stress of humans in every pocket of nature has impacted animal territory, lowering the number of reproducing females each year.

And then when you consider the odd tourist that approaches and causes an animal to be relocated or killed—improper wildlife tourism.

→ What You Can Do Instead

Knowing that humans and wildlife don't mix for the better, do your part to give wildlife all the distance it needs in every situation. There are very few encounters in the wild that animals initiate themselves. It can be very tempting to prompt an interaction but fight that urge.

When booking a tour or planning a day of wildlife experiences, do the following:

- research the operator and area you'll be visiting in advance
- take the time to know the laws and recommendations around wildlife encounters
- do not feed wildlife
- never get between a baby and its mother
- keep wildlife wild

We love getting into nature on road trips. For my family this means hiking, kayaking, and beach days. We are careful to practice wildlife distancing and to teach our kids the value in keeping wildlife wild.

GOING GREEN AND AVOIDING
SINGLE-USE PLASTIC

Going zero-waste at home is very simple and can be done through a few key changes to how grocery and home shopping is done. When packing for a road trip, it can be much more difficult to purchase snacks, supplies, and souvenirs without generating waste with each bite or use.

Simple ways to avoid creating plastic waste as a tourist are:

- travel with reusable supplies: metal straws, bamboo cutlery, refillable water bottles
- bring your own soap products
- only use hotel-provided products wrapped in paper (bar of soap vs. small body wash bottle)
- use for-here mugs/cups instead of taking beverages to go

Spending ten minutes before you head out on a road trip getting your own supplies together is very doable. And if each person traveling took an extra moment to be thoughtful, millions of pieces of single-use plastic could be avoided.

Low-impact tourism isn't a huge shift for most and doesn't compromise the experience. By choosing to not create waste or to opt for the path of least impact and minimize your own carbon footprint, you'll be making a difference. By understanding how you impact the wildlife and world around you, you can make sustainable tourism the norm and ensure that the next generation has the same travel opportunities and experiences you've had.

IDEAS AND THEMES FOR UNFORGETTABLE ROAD TRIPS

You can always just hop in the car and see what happens. You might start driving and see a million beautiful sights or end up somewhere you never want to leave. Or you might start a road trip with a goal, theme, or an idea of the types of experiences you want to enjoy.

And that's what we're going to conquer now. Planning a road trip with a theme in mind is a great way to drive your itinerary and ensure you're seeking out unusual opportunities. I find that when we travel with a theme it helps us to enjoy our trips more because then we've built in conversations comparing the experiences we've had along the way. And education? Yes! Themed trips with kids are amazing learning tools.

As you read on, remember that any of these themes can be morphed to fit your road trip crew. Don't pigeonhole your travels into a narrow path.

IDEAS FOR SOLO TRAVEL ROAD TRIPS

I've always loved solo road trips. I love my family and the adventures we have together, but man oh man, there's nothing quite like the freedom of the open road and nobody else to worry about.

Epic Photo Journey

I love the idea of hitting the road with just my camera and a basic plan. Doing an Epic Photo Journey road trip can happen nearly anywhere. On the West Coast, heading across the mountains to the desert landscapes full of buttes and canyons is a surefire way to capture unbelievable contrast in your photography. The sunrises leave you speechless and the sunsets are full of color from the dust in the air.

If you're more of a mountain-goer, there are many routes across the Rockies, Cascades, and Sierras that will wow you. The joy of doing a solo road trip up in the mountains is that you can push your limits and venture onto ridgeline gravel roads and jackknife highways that you may not feel comfortable doing with others.

Are you a weather chaser? If you're planning a solo road trip in the right season, you may have the opportunity to set up your camera and just wait for storms to roll by. Having the freedom of only having to worry about yourself gives you the chance to sit, enjoy the earth, and photograph whatever inspires you.

Destination Suggestions: Eastern Washington to the Columbia River Gorge, Central Oregon, the eastern side of the Sierras (California), Beartooth Highway (Montana), Tornado Alley (Oklahoma, Nebraska, Kansas), Florida Birding Trail.

Hikes Nobody Else Will Do

Am I the only one that likes hikes that start with a ridiculous climb and have zero people along the trail? Or to put a kayak in the water and not have a scheduled return time? Solo road trips, whether for a day or a week, are my chance to do those hikes and paddles.

Make special hikes your theme for a road trip. You'll need to plan and prep differently for a hiking-themed trip over a beach-themed itinerary, and you may need to get yourself in better shape before you do it, but it's well worth the consideration.

Destination Suggestions: North Cascades (Washington), Joshua Tree National Park (California), Voyageurs National Park for kayaking (Minnesota), the Appalachian Trail (Georgia, North Carolina, Tennessee, New Hampshire), Everglades National Park (Florida).

Historic Routes

Why are historic routes included in solo road trips? Have you intentionally done a historic route with a significant other? Unless you're both big history buffs or have the same level of patience, planning a road trip to follow a historic route can be a challenge.

Of course, today there are many more sights and activities along well-known historic routes, but if you're sticking to a theme and making stops at each historic marker or museum, it can wear on a person.

Having said that, pick a historic route and have a blast nerding out! I really love road trips through the mountains because it's historically mining country. They provide beautiful scenery, lots of museums typically, rock-hounding (searching for special rocks and minerals out in nature), and plenty of unique tours. The mountains of Georgia and Idaho are two really interesting, and often overlooked, road trip destinations.

Another historic theme is pioneer trails. While pioneer trails are mostly located in the west, they had to come from somewhere! The Oregon (Missouri to Oregon), Applegate (Nevada to Oregon), Mormon (Illinois to Utah), and Pony Express Trails cover diverse territory and offer different perspectives of history.

More Route Suggestions: Civil Rights Trail (Washington, DC, to Alabama), Route 30 (Oregon), Route 66 (Illinois to California), National Votes for Women Trail (New York).

Finding All the Food Trucks

One of the greatest developments of the twenty-first century is the popularity of the food truck. They're mobile, they embody unique cuisines, and they're all over! Even our neighborhood here in St. Augustine, Florida, has its own food truck culture. Just our neighborhood. And it's part of a bigger food truck culture in the city, which in turn is also found to the north in Jacksonville and to the south in Daytona.

Florida doesn't hold a monopoly on food-truck towns. Texas, Washington, California, and Indiana are food truck paradise as well. So, how do you turn this into a road trip plan? Easy-peasy.

Here's how you make a food truck–themed road trip:

1. Choose a region with a few good-sized towns or cities
2. Search "food trucks in _____ (city name)" for each major stop
3. Build your route allowing you at least two meals in each food truck hub
4. Mix interesting sights and cultural spots into the plan
5. Hit the road and eat!

Did you ever think traveling with the idea of trying lots of different food trucks would be something you'd want to do? It's such a great way to experience local cultures and support small businesses while you travel.

Destination Suggestions: Pacific Northwest, California beach communities, Southeastern Texas Loop (Houston to San Antonio to Austin to Dallas), National Capital Region.

COUPLES ON THE ROAD: REKINDLING FUN TOGETHER

I sometimes think back to before we had kids and get a sense of nostalgia. I remember how we would go camping at a moment's notice or would drive through the night to get someplace extra early. I also think back to road trips I would *never* take the kids on, either for safety or ridiculousness. These suggested themes are fun and offer plenty of quiet time together.

Lighthouses and Sleepy Towns

The US and Canada have so many lighthouses that putting together a road trip plan to visit them is very easy. Did you know that some of the most beautiful lighthouses in North America are actually located on the Great

Lakes? That's right, you can do a lighthouse road trip starting in Milwaukee and circle Lake Michigan.

And with lighthouses often come sleepy nautical towns, sometimes still bustling, but often still set back in the days of small-boat fishing. There's nothing quite as romantic as strolling the streets of a town you swear is the set of a Hallmark movie.

Another reason lighthouse road trips make for great couple adventures is for the lodging. Where you find lighthouses you also find bed and breakfasts. The Pacific Northwest, Great Lakes, and Northeast all have a remarkable number of B&Bs in their nautical towns. They are a wonderful romantic option, and often have just enough quirkiness that you'll find yourself laughing together over stories of doilies at your grandmother's house when you were a kid.

Destination Suggestions: San Juan Island Hopping (Washington), Oregon Coast, Upper Peninsula (Michigan), Lake Erie Shore (Ohio, Pennsylvania, New York), Nautical New England (Maine, New Hampshire, Massachusetts).

Wine Country Exploration

I never met a wine country I didn't love. Wine country road trips are wonderful for couples, both young and old, for a variety of reasons:

- beautiful scenery
- lots of outdoor activities
- cute towns with unique accommodations
- lots of wine

If you're not into wine as a topic of interest or education, that's okay. Visiting wineries is an opportunity to learn together and broaden your knowledge or palate. And if that doesn't sound fun, then just know that there are amazing restaurants in nearly every wine region.

If wine isn't your thing, wine country also tends to be full of orchards and hop fields. That means there are also cideries and breweries. And bakeries. There's something for everyone in wine country, even if you don't enjoy adult beverages.

PS: You don't have to travel to Napa, California, to do a wine country road trip. Did you know that wine grapes are grown in all forty-eight of the lower US? Each province of Canada grows wine grapes too! And Mexico even has some wine regions.

Suggested Destinations: Yakima Valley (Washington), Willamette Valley (Oregon), Ozark Highlands (Missouri), Loudoun County (Virginia), and the Hamptons or Upstate New York.

Views that Inspire Romance

You've got a week on the road with your significant other. You can't agree on a theme or what activities you're both interested in, but you might agree that each day you can find an Inspiration Point. You know, a place with a view so beautiful that you're taken aback and have to enjoy the moment like there's nothing else in the world.

Okay, maybe that doesn't sound ideal or sounds too much like "young love," but it's a great road trip theme! Planning a trip where you can end each day with a stunning view is easier than it sounds.

As you build your itinerary, make sure that each day includes an exceptional viewpoint. That could be a sunset hike (safety first, be prepared), starting your day watching the sun come up over a valley, lunch looking out over the ocean . . . There are many ways to enjoy beautiful views.

Besides inspiring romance or being left in awe, what's the purpose in finding these views? I'm glad you asked. Enjoying a mutual view brings people together. Sure, there's the moment everyone has to take a photo or video, but after that, it's just you two and the view. It's a moment to be quiet and appreciate each other *and* the adventure you're on together.

Suggested Destinations: Utah's Canyon Country, Southwest Texas

Sunsets, Blue Ridge Mountains (Tennessee), Door County (Wisconsin), Florida's Gulf Coast.

Movie Location Scavenger Hunt

The reason movie locations is a couples theme and not a family theme is simple: not enough kids care deeply about the movies of the 1980s and '90s, which make for the best movie-themed road trips. True, there are lots of movies kids enjoy and they very well might recognize locations, but this is a chance to, as a couple, lose yourselves in movie nostalgia.

The most obvious choice for doing a movie-themed road trip is to head to Vancouver, BC, aka Hollywood North. The whole area is basically a familiar movie set, from *Jumanji* to *The NeverEnding Story*. Even the small towns surrounding Vancouver are frequent filming locations and have been for decades.

The other obvious choice (and truly it's a good one) is driving from Las Vegas to Los Angeles. This road trip is fun with kids too. Even without researching filming sites, the drive from the Las Vegas Strip to Hollywood Boulevard is full of iconic shots, and you don't even have to wander far off course.

Suggested Routes: New York City to Washington, DC, Exploring Chicago, San Francisco Bay Area, Hipster Portland (Oregon), Hallmark Movies, and *The Walking Dead* (Georgia).

FAMILY TRAVEL THEMES

My favorite thing about being a dad is getting to share my love of travel with my kids. They love it too, whether we're flying or driving from point A to point B. When we plan family trips, they love to help choose what adventures we are going to have. Family road trips are so special and truly are at the heart of countless childhood memories for so many.

National Parks and Junior Rangers

Before I go any further, did you know that adults can complete Junior Ranger programs within national parks? And you even get to earn the badge! Now that you have that nugget of information, how excited are you to start planning a few national park road trips?!

While some national parks have become extremely popular in recent years, there are still many that remain rather undiscovered. The most popular parks, like Yellowstone and Zion National Parks, are very well developed both outside and within the borders of the park. Parks like these are easy to add to a road trip plan because there are ample hotels to choose from, so camping is just an option versus being required.

Some other national parks are more remote and aren't built up the way more established parks are. For example, Wrangell-St. Elias National Park in Alaska is *not* close to any major cities or roadways, but the adventure of getting there is remarkable, and the nature is unmatched. Adding Wrangell to an Alaskan adventure ensures that you'll be able to see more of the state than Anchorage and the well-developed corridor leading to Denali National Park.

Note: There are many state parks and Bureau of Land Management sights that rival the views, hikes, and history of national parks. When you're planning your national park road trip, *do not overlook these places*!

As you start to research and plan, take into consideration the popularity of national parks for family travel in terms of scheduling. When school lets out the crowds increase, as happens on weekends as well. It'll still be fun, but not as calm and with potentially less active wildlife.

Suggested Destinations: National Parks in the Sierras of California, Olympic National Park Loop Drive (Washington), Shenandoah National Park (Virginia), Colorado Parks.

Amusement Parks for Miles

One easy way to make an amusement park vacation more budget friendly is to drive there instead of flying. With the cost per person to travel being so much less, you'll have more to spend on park tickets and experiences.

There are more amusement parks than just Disney Parks, and they are quite easy to add to the same trip plan. Also, if you're not on one of the coasts, there are some pretty epic theme parks in the Midwest and Texas.

These clusters can be added to the same trips if you're looking for non-stop park fun:

- Southern California: Disneyland and Disney California Adventure, Universal Studios Hollywood, Knott's Berry Farm, Six Flags Magic Mountain, LEGOLAND California
- Florida Fun: Universal Studios and Islands of Adventure, Walt Disney World (four parks), Busch Gardens (Tampa), LEGOLAND Florida
- Eastern US Parks: Six Flags Great Adventure (New Jersey), Hershey Park (Pennsylvania), Cedar Point and Kings Island (Ohio), loop back to Busch Gardens Williamsburg (Virginia)

Everyone has a different goal with family vacations, so if amusement parks are your thing, go for it! To ensure that nobody gets burned out or suffers from roller coaster fatigue, be sure to mix in some relaxation time or other sorts of nature/culture into the trip.

Digging into History

Like with the historic route theme discussed in the solo travel section, digging into history with kids can be a mixed bag. Some kids get so into it and others couldn't care less. We've discovered some key activities and sights to make historic travel family friendly.

When you're planning a historic destinations trip, look for opportunities to take part in living history or reenactments. This is a great way to generate interest and give context to the history everyone is learning about. Depending on the age of the kids, sometimes you can even be involved in different historic activities.

Another way to approach a trip through history is by looking through the lens of current or recent history. While there may not be designated trails (historic travel routes) to follow, you can make requests in advance to visit the national or state capitol buildings and, in some cases, even get to watch history be made on the floor of the Senate or House.

Every family is unique and will have a different take on how to plan a history-themed trip, and it very well may not be for everyone. In any case, a little bit of research goes a long way and making a learning experience from a family vacation is always a good idea.

Suggested Destinations: Virginia's Historic Triangle; Washington, DC; Civil Rights in Alabama; El Camino Real (California); Lewis and Clark Trail (Missouri to Oregon).

Science and Dinosaurs

"Geology rocks!" That will forever be my favorite dad joke. And I use it every day, even when we're at home. North America has some really fascinating places to explore when it comes to geology.

Yellowstone really does live up to the hype and yes, it really is a trip that you should plan with your family at some point. You've got eighteen summers with kids, I'm sure that at least one of those could include a road trip to Wyoming. And Yellowstone National Park really is more than its incredible geology. The wildlife, being able to see scientific methods at work with the reintroduction of wolves, being able to observe weather patterns in one afternoon, observing the water cycle through geysers . . . So much science, so little time!

Another incredible place to observe science is Central Florida. Most people think of Florida as being nothing but beaches and theme parks, and while those are elements of the Sunshine State, the true gems are the freshwater springs. Florida has more than one thousand freshwater springs. While some are located in city or state parks, others are on private property with camping nearby. Their consistent water temperatures are home to thousands of manatees in the winter months, and kayakers and alligators in the summer.

If you haven't noticed, there are many road trip themes that venture through upstate New York. There is science to behold up in the Finger Lakes region with more than fifty significant waterfalls. From Watkins Glen State Park to High Falls in the middle of the city of Rochester, you can visit several waterfalls each day, hike or stroll, and observe erosion and wildlife with every step.

For one more really cool, really fun idea, consider a dinosaur-themed road trip. Believe it or not, there are a few places around the US with quite the concentration of fossils. Utah and Montana come to mind for witnessing active dig sites, but did you know that Ohio and Oregon are known for their fossil deposits too? Even Los Angeles has an incredible active dig site *directly in the city*.

Suggested Destinations: Central Montana, Eastern Oregon, Ohio and Indiana, Denver Area.

FAVORITE FAMILY THEME EVER: EPIC TOWERING TREES

I can't even count how many road trips we've done as a family, but I can tell you which was my favorite. We went with the theme of Epic Towering Trees. Living on the West Coast, evergreens are all around. These include Douglas fir forests in Washington, pines in Oregon, and sequoias and redwoods in California.

We made the trek to Sequoia National Park in the late spring, expecting hot days and unforgettable hikes. What we experienced was an impromptu blizzard and unpassable trails. We waited it out, though, and were able to enjoy the vibrant red sequoia trees against the fresh snow. In Kings Canyon National Park, we had the same thing. Walking through fallen tree tunnels, tromping through slush while groves of trees (so epic that they all have names) towered above us.

We continued on to Yosemite National Park, which is well known for its sheer granite cliffs, but also for its own groves of sequoias. Visiting the trees and then seeking out our own quiet side of the park, in the Hetch Hetchy Valley, we enjoyed the best of both worlds: giant forests and raging waterfalls.

From there we hit the coast. Just out of San Francisco we came to Muir Woods National Monument. Talk about epic trees! So epic it felt like we were on the Forest Moon of Endor. Wait, what? Yes, these forests were home to the Ewoks and were the filming location for *Return of the Jedi*. We mixed a movie theme into our tree theme. Genius, if I do say so myself.

After some time exploring the Bay Area National Parks and trees, we continued up the coast, eventually landing in Redwoods National and State Parks. Too long in the mountains was wearing on us "coasties," so getting to the redwoods that basically grow from the beach up into the hills was refreshing.

Besides the incredible groves of trees and ample hiking opportunities, we found some picturesque small towns to explore. Bodega Bay (where they filmed *The Birds*), Eureka and its colorful Victorians, and Fort Bragg with its beach culture made for an incredible finish to our trip. We got to visit lighthouses and eat our way up the California coast (FYI: mashed potato cones with gravy instead of ice cream with chocolate sauce are a thing).

We rounded out our Epic Towering Trees road trip with a stay in a log cabin chateau. At Oregon Caves National Monument, instead of having a national park lodge like most other parks, it has a chateau built from roughly hewn logs. As if staying in the most rustic accommodations wasn't enough, the Oregon Caves were right outside our door and were perfect for exploring with kids.

Can you see why this is my favorite family road trip we've ever done? Such a mix of sights and activities, and all of it on one itinerary. In retrospect, we could've broken this trip up into three separate adventures, but if you're going to go epic, go really epic with the road trip.

GETTING KIDS INVOLVED
IN TRAVEL PLANNING

I actually get a lot of questions about having the kids help us plan our vacations and road trips. Yes, our boys (six and nine years old) have opinions and interests and it's extremely important that we consider those when vacation planning. The best road trips will no doubt have lots of points of interest, but some will be more exciting than others depending on your family. We've certainly had some great ones . . . and some duds.

If you've got kids, you have an opportunity to show them that you value their opinions and interests by getting them involved with planning a trip. We like to use travel books or multipage atlases for the kids to browse through. We've done this for a few years now where each kid picks a trip or some sights they think would be the most interesting to them. As we schedule future travel, we incorporate their requests and sometimes even let them pick the destination outright.

Of course, as an adult, you have to keep in mind things like budgets and your life calendar, but empowering kids to share what drives them and inspires their minds will launch incredible, meaningful road trips they'll remember long into adulthood.

CHAPTER 2

PACKING

VERSATILE ROAD TRIP GEAR

While it would be great to be able to just hop in the car and go (which I guess you could very well do), it's always nice to be well equipped for both fun and comfort. I don't mean that you need to have all the comforts of home with you, but you should definitely be well prepared.

And let's face it: traveling with some conveniences makes a long trip smoother and more enjoyable. I've broken this section down into two groups of road trip essentials: conveniences and organization.

ROAD TRIP CONVENIENCES

I'm a sucker for making life easier, and that includes adding conveniences to long car trips with kids. I'm not going to tell you how to manage your family but learn from my experience when I say that cold snacks and useful gadgets make for a lovely trip.

Power Converter

I still don't know why all cars aren't made with standard electrical outlets; it seems like such a basic requirement these days. Fortunately, if your car doesn't have a built-in outlet, there is a solution. A power converter is almost a necessity these days, particularly for those who are traveling while working. Working on the road is possible because of these helpful converters.

What is a power converter? A power converter is a device that makes a twelve-volt plug (a cigarette lighter socket) usable with standard house plugs. You plug it into a twelve-volt outlet, and then you can plug a regular two- or three-prong plug into it. We have one that has two standard outlets and two high-speed USB charging ports. This is perfect for keeping our laptop, phones, and tablets charged. We don't use things like curling or flattening irons, but I hear it's great to be able to use those on the road too.

Note: Running a power converter while the vehicle isn't running may drain the battery. This is more so a solution to provide electricity while driving. It's perfect to allow a passenger to work on a laptop while covering lots of miles.

Travel Pillows

Have you ever looked back at your kids in the car on a long road trip only to find them asleep and slumped over? We finally found a great travel pillow for the kids that helps them fall asleep and stay upright. The kids love them so much that they also use them in the house when watching movies! The pillow is designed to wrap around the neck and buttons closed to keep the structure, supporting the head but not restricting movement or airways. When you're looking for a good travel pillow, seek out one with the feature of a button or snap to maintain structure.

For us grown-ups, we need something a little bigger. The option I've found to be the most comfortable, and which I've used in the car and on international flights, is a foam one. The memory foam is quite firm, and there is a clip to keep it in place. These elements are what make it really effective for adults on car trips. Shop for one that connects in the front and you'll love the comfort and support.

In any case, when you're shopping for a neck pillow, look for the key features of firmness and the ability to secure it in place. They're never too big to bring in the car and you'll be so glad to have one come mile four hundred.

Iceless Cooler

We like to pack a lot of fruits, vegetables, and cheese slices for road trip snacks. Not only are these great healthy options for the entire family but they're also eco-friendly options. We precut carrots, cucumbers, bell peppers, cheese, etc. and put them in storage containers in our iceless cooler. We also like cold water, so it's great to put our water bottles in the cooler to keep cold.

When you're done driving for the day, you can still use your cooler if you've got the adapter that lets you also plug the cooler into a standard outlet. This has been great for hotel rooms without a mini fridge. Note: I bring both this small cooler for the main area of the car and a larger cooler for the actual lunch supplies and additional snack/meal items on road trips, and I recommend you do too.

Tablets Preloaded with Apps/Entertainment

Sure, a tablet seems like a no-brainer, but one that has been thoughtfully curated is key. A selection of games and movies or shows makes for a nice mix. And don't forget to include a book or two. This is good for both kids *and* adults.

When it comes to movies, the lower the quality picture, the smaller the download. That said, for the kids, the lower quality isn't noticeable, so we can store lots of movies on their tablets. We like the Kindle products for their price point and battery life. Apple and Samsung products also work well, but we've found the Kindle line to last longer with kids (and there are kid-specific options).

Headphones

Do you want silence in your car sometimes? Make sure to pack headphones! We really limit screen time for the kids at home, but on long road trips we feel it's okay to let the boys watch feature-length movies or play a variety of games. Headphones designed for kids are great because they are sized appropriately and usually have a volume control switch on the cord.

Adult passengers will usually have figured out their favorite headphones, but if it's up for discussion or shopping, finding a pair that also has noise-canceling features can be really beneficial for naps on road trips.

KEEPING THE CAR ORGANIZED

Nothing stresses me out more on a road trip than a messy, cluttered car where I can't find things. After a few days of things not being put back where they were initially packed and sand and rocks being tracked in, I'm at the end of my car-clutter rope.

With enough trips, though, our family has figured out what works to keep things put together and clean over a lot of hours in the car.

Kids Travel Trays

This is an essential road trip item for kids. Our kids love to have a lot of different activities. Having a travel tray that folds up to contain all their activities has proven helpful to keeping organized time and again.

We've tried several and found a favorite that comes with several different activity sheets. These sheets can be reused because they slide under the plastic cover. Kids use dry-erase markers to either color or complete mazes or crosswords and just erase the marker when they're done. They also just like to draw on a blank space too.

The different activity trays we've tried all have side pouches that make great places to store the markers and other small toys like LEGOs, minifigures, Pokémon cards, or whatever treasures they must bring with them on trips.

This tray also has a place for a tablet to rest too. We've found that our kids get carsick if they hold their tablets. They haven't gotten carsick since using travel trays! Their benefits are endless.

When you're shopping for travel trays, inquire at your local toy or educational store. You can also search online for options. Do a search for "kids travel tray" and you'll find many versions to choose from.

Car Vacuum

Okay, so I don't know about you, but I hate sand and dirt. I know that a lot of dirt will be tracked into the car during our road trips. We're always hiking in the woods or playing on the beach, and all of this gets tracked into the car. In order to keep myself sane, I just need to be able to do some quick cleaning along the way. Also, you never know when that box of goldfish crackers will take a tumble and then the kids step all over them, making a crumb disaster.

You'll be thankful to have a vacuum on hand to clean up the known and unplanned messes. Most compact car vacuums plug into a twelve-volt outlet and have enough strength for cleaning up on the go.

While it may seem unimportant initially, after a few days of accumulation, you'll be beyond thankful to be able to quickly spot-vacuum the car.

Cleaning Supplies

Tissues, baby wipes, napkins . . . Find me a road trip where you don't need to clean something up within the first hour and I'll find you a magical dragon to fly you to your next destination. Packing a cleaning supply bundle is just smart planning.

We've found that baby wipes serve a million purposes, but disinfecting wipes are excellent too. Wipes paired with paper towels or napkins can keep your car and passengers *not* sticky and much more sanitary over the duration of a trip.

Air Fresheners

Yes, this is important. Even if you're good about removing trash and cleaning up the car each day, the smell of tired people and stale clothing isn't pleasant and develops quickly. Since everyone has a different level of sensitivity, you may need to try a few options to get your odor-fighting process figured out.

Actual vehicle air fresheners, such as the ones you hang from your mirror or clip onto a vent, may be very overpowering and nauseating. If it's just you on the road trip and you don't mind that, go for it. There's your solution.

If there are more people traveling with you, consider an odor-eliminating canister. These types of products can easily be adjusted to limit the amount of scent coming from them, and because they're typically stored out of sight, they're much more subtle, yet still effective.

My preferred method for keeping the car fresh is an odor-eliminating spray at the end of each day. Spraying down the seats and floor with a light mist can really do wonders, and if you do it at the end of the day, that will give it time to do its job and also lose any overwhelming smell overnight.

Top pick: Citrus or orange vehicle spray. It tends to be more powerful immediately but dissipates into a pleasant hint of the aroma. Citrus is very effective.

Natural alternative: A citrus or lemongrass essential oil will also do the trick. You can make your own air freshening cloth by applying a fair amount of an essential oil to it, and then store it in your glove box or console, bringing it out to wipe things down at the end of each day.

PREPAREDNESS PACKING LIST

Yes, fun and adventures and beautiful sights await you on your road trip, but so do other random, unplanned experiences. Just in case, you'll need to pack your vehicle to make sure you're prepared.

First-Aid Kit

Road trips are much more than sitting in a car, and that includes hiking and beach time. You really do never know what's going to cause an injury

or wound. Packing a first-aid kit should be a basic step to road trip prep, whether you're traveling with kids or not. I feel like us adults get injured more often than the kids.

An ideal road trip first-aid kit will include, at minimum:

- bandages of all sizes
- antibacterial ointment
- gauze
- Ace bandage

If you want to add bonus items, include burn gel, sunscreen, bug spray, anti-itch cream, and pain reliever. Think about travel experiences you've had before and what you've wished you had on the road. Put those things in your first-aid kit.

Snow Chains

Yes, it's worth it to invest in snow chains unless you know beyond a shadow of a doubt that you won't have any potential of coming in contact with snow. You need to consider both the season you're taking a road trip in *and* the environment you're visiting. Just because you don't expect snow doesn't mean it won't happen.

Tales from the Road: Picture it: July 5, it's a beautiful, hot day exploring Yellowstone National Park. Rain moves in, we go to bed, and it gets quiet around 2:00 a.m. Seven a.m. rolls around and the kids are awake . . . and Yellowstone is covered in snow. Yes, July 6 and snow was the order for the day. We used chains until we got to plowed roads and we stayed safe. The big bonus of the experience, though, was getting to see herds of bison covered in snow, plowing their way through the meadows.

Simple Tool Kit

You're on a road trip. You don't want to fix things, but the random vehicle or equipment malfunction totally happens. From loose kayak racks to wheel-well flaps dangling from the car, you never know what mishaps a road trip may bring. I always doublé-check my tool kit before leaving our house for a long trip. My kit isn't fancy, but it's got some important tools in it:

- a variety of screwdrivers
- zip ties
- a carpet cutter/blade
- pliers and crescent wrench
- twine/rope
- socket wrench kit (metric)
- battery head cleaner (bristled brush)

While you might look at this list and think you'll never need any of these things, you very well might, even if it's not for its intended purpose. Bring a tool kit; you'll be glad you did.

Roadside Emergency Kit

Throughout this road trip survival guide you'll see continual reference to a roadside emergency kit. That's because roadside emergencies happen all the time, and while sometimes they are just small ones, they can be serious nonetheless.

Take the time before hitting the road to actually confirm that you're well prepared for an emergency. Your roadside kit should include:

- jumper cables
- at least three flares
- reflective triangles or small cones
- first-aid kit
- flashlight

- backup charger (for cell phone)
- nonperishable snacks
- drinking water
- water for vehicle engine
- lighter or matches
- paper map of the general area

I like to take the approach of being more prepared than not enough. I can't imagine you'd want to be underprepared, so take the time to look out for the worst-case scenario.

SIMPLE ROAD TRIP PACKING LISTS

Let's make this simple (because you have numerous complications in life and putting together a successful trip is enough work). Packing lists: Everybody has them, nobody uses them. But that changes right now.

It can be frustrating to be on the road and realize you forgot your favorite flip-flops or that you didn't actually pack a jacket (I've done that more than once). While packing may be a no-brainer, it never hurts to use a well-thought-out list as a safety net.

SIMPLE PACKING LISTS FOR EVERYONE

Can we agree that everyone needs to bring a toothbrush? Yes. And shoes too. Simple as those things may be, both are really easy to leave the house without.

You know, you're rushing and getting the car ready to go by a certain time, you've been wearing your slippers, you finish packing and you take off! . . . You're still wearing your slippers, not shoes, and you were so busy you didn't brush your teeth and your toothbrush is still sitting on the bathroom counter.

Now that you get it, here's your list so you can hit the road with confidence. And if you need any of these items on your day of departure, pack a version you can use on the road so it's done in advance versus forgetting it the day you leave.

Travel Basics

Any road trip packing should include all of these items. And yes, flip-flops are even useful during winter travel. These are the absolute basics (besides clothing):

- itinerary/travel plan
- phone charger
- sneakers/tennis shoes
- flip-flops/sandals
- hat or cap
- light jacket
- sunglasses
- reusable water bottle (one per person)
- large picnic blanket or sheet
- power bank with cords
- camera (see below for full camera packing list)
- notepad with pen
- first-aid kit
- lighter or matches (can be in emergency kit)
- travel pillow/neck pillow
- quick-drying towels (for swimming or hiking)
- emergency radio (because you never know)

Bathroom/Personal Items

You may have a whole toiletry routine you do each day, and if you want to continue that while you're on the road, go for it. But also consider a journey of discovery, such as a road trip, an opportunity to leave daily life and expectations behind. Perhaps you can skip makeup for a week or maybe let your beard grow out . . .

- toothbrush and toothpaste
- eco-friendly soap products
- shaving supplies
- contact solution/glasses
- deodorant
- hair care/hairbrush
- skin care/moisturizer
- sunblock

If you take a daily supplement or medications, be sure to pack those as well. Separating out what you need for the trip or the amount for the time leading up to the trip will allow you to pack these important items in advance, ensuring they aren't left behind.

PACKING FOR KIDS ON THE ROAD

Even the easiest kiddos have specific needs when they're away from home. I'm not saying you need to pack up the whole playroom but bringing items that will make the trip easier or more pleasant for everyone in the car is smart.

Treat a road trip with small kids like a visit to the doctor where you will be in the waiting room for a loooong time. You need options that are fun, interesting, and can hold their attention. Also, consider what brings your child comfort, not just entertainment.

- stuffed friends (up to three)
- travel tray (flat surface)
- coloring supplies

- tablet with downloads and charging cable
- headphones
- comfort items (blanky, lucky toy, etc.)
- nightlight

Parents, you know your kids best. Packing in a minimalist way will prevent both excess clutter on your road trip and get your kids more engaged with you on the drive. And the reason I recommend limiting the number of stuffies kids bring on a road trip is because the more you bring, the easier it is to lose one.

One final thing to consider is white noise. You can pack a sound machine or just download an app onto your phone or tablet but adding white noise to your nightly environment can really help kids adjust and get good sleep on road trips. Staying someplace different each night can be weird for kids, so adding a familiar sound element can really help.

THINGS TO BRING INTO NATURE

Road trips are a wonderful way to get out in nature. I like to include several days out in the woods or hiking whenever I'm planning a driving vacation, even if our primary destination is a city or theme park.

You don't need to pack full-on survival supplies and backwoods gear, but a little bit of thoughtful outdoor equipment will be appreciated when the time comes.

Useful Outdoor Gear

The following are useful items to bring for basic outdoor exploring. It's better to be prepared than wishing you had packed more thoughtfully. Unless your primary travel plan is canyoning or whitewater kayaking, the following list should keep you from overpacking, yet you'll still be prepared to explore the outdoors:

- binoculars
- hiking shoes (doesn't have to be boots)
- small backpack
- bug spray
- wildlife identification guide

Again, this list is minimal because we're not talking about a full-on camping trip. If you choose not to pack the few extras for outdoor activities, that's okay, but be sure to tally up the number of times on your trip you wish you would've had X, Y, and Z with you . . .

Camera Equipment for the Road

Photography means something different to everyone. For a hobbyist, they might see a road trip as the perfect time to use all the camera gear they've ever purchased. If you're a professional, you know what you need and what you don't. And for the amateur photographer, well, what should you actually be bringing along?

This photography gear list is for the amateur or aspiring professional. The following equipment is good for capturing your experience and getting photographs or video that you'll actually be able to use for fun projects or just to add to your collection. If you're new to photography, this list may seem like a bit much, but really, these are the basics if you're looking for a good, uncomplicated camera kit:

- DSLR or mirrorless camera
- telephoto lens
- wide-angle lens
- tripod with mount
- lens cloths
- camera battery charger

- spare memory card
- camera bag or backpack

This basic camera packing list should get any amateur photographer through a good trip. With bringing backup memory cards and just the basic lenses, you can successfully shoot nearly any scenario.

And yes, the tripod really is necessary. If you're using the telephoto for photographing far-away wildlife, stabilization is key. If you need to document that you and your crew are having the time of your lives, set up the tripod and timer and you can actually be in a group photo. See, everything serves a purpose.

To be clear, camera phones today are remarkable and take incredible photos. If you don't have the DSLR gear or don't want to invest, that's fine. Before you hit the road, I'd recommend reading a few online articles to get the latest tech tips for using your phone camera to its maximum potential.

SMART CLOTHING LIST

I will forever overpack when it comes to clothing, unless of course I follow my list. Yes, I want to be prepared. No, I'm not going to wear all five pairs of pants I packed . . . because I only like two of them.

You already have enough other stuff to bring along on your road trip, so when you're packing clothes for a multiday adventure, just be honest with yourself about what you'll actually use. More than that, luggage takes up a lot of space in the car, so bringing fewer clothes leaves more room in the back. This in turn allows you to keep the main seating areas in your vehicle cleaner and more organized.

To make it easier, here are two lists: one for cold, wet-weather trips and the other for sunny, warm destinations.

Cold-Weather Trip Clothes

Always look at the forecast before you leave on a road trip and pack clothing that matches it, adding a few pieces that you'd use if the weather gets way worse or significantly better.

Be honest with yourself as you pack. If you're road-tripping through rural America or are heading deep into the mountains of Canada, do you really need to look your finest at all times, or can you sport the same jeans a few times?

This is for a seven-day trip, fall weather, equal parts outdoors and civilization:

- pants—three pairs
- shorts—one pair
- shirts—seven
- swimwear—one
- sweater/pullover—two
- socks and underwear—seven sets
- thick/wool socks—two pairs
- sleepwear—three sets
- warm, weatherproof jacket
- gloves and scarf

Sticking with this minimal but smart packing list will provide for more space in your vehicle while still making sure that you're well prepared for a variety of weather. Of course, update this packing list as you see fit, but try to keep the number of items you bring to a minimum.

Warm and Sunny Road Trip Clothing

I love packing for hot-weather trips because it's so easy. A little of this, a little of that, maybe buy a souvenir tank top somewhere if I need to . . .

Warm-weather trips often include hiking and swimming, so packing clothes that are versatile in any type of weather is smart! I'd love to say that weather reports will always be accurate and never change, but that's not realistic. Be practical with your packing to ensure the best experiences:

- shorts—three pairs
- pants—one pair
- shirts/tanks—seven
- sweater/pullover—one
- socks and underwear—seven sets
- thick/wool socks—two pairs (if hiking)
- sleepwear—three sets
- light jacket

It pays to check the weather forecast for the days leading up to your trip so you can understand the weather patterns and prepare appropriately. You can pack in advance, and if you think you haven't packed the right clothes, you can always grab that one extra item you're worried will make or break your trip.

CAR ORGANIZATION

There's a lot to be said about celebrating the people who are good at getting/staying organized. I wish that was me all of the time, but to be honest, it's not. I have my systems in place that help me clear up my disorganization in my daily life, but there are times when I fail. *But* . . . not when it comes to organizing the car for road trips.

FIVE EASY STEPS TO
AN ORGANIZED VEHICLE

You have to start somewhere, and setting yourself up for success on the road begins with creating a road trip–ready vehicle. In the days leading up to your big road trip, you've got all sorts of prep to do. One of the most important, if not *the* most important, things to do is pack the car.

When we go camping we have to be super specific in how we load our gear, because camping gear can be very large. For a standard road trip, we can be a bit looser, but still need to be deliberate in our packing choices.

A Fresh Palette: Clean Out the Car

Start here. No questions. Before you start outfitting your vehicle to be an adventure mobile, you need to clean out any accumulation from everyday life.

This means that you walk out to your car with a box and a garbage bag and remove everything. Yes, some items may end up right back inside, but starting completely fresh will really help. Stuff you want to keep goes into the box to be organized later, and then trash and mysterious items go into the garbage bag for disposal.

Don't overlook the nooks and crannies:

- glove box
- center console
- door bins
- seatback pockets
- under the seats
- armrest bins (some cars)
- trunk/rear of vehicle

Items that you know are going right back into the car you set to the side. This might include vehicle manuals, snow chains, emergency kit, etc.

Actually Clean the Car

You've emptied your vehicle and all that's left is sand and cookie crumbs (and handprints on the windows). Let's get all of that cleaned up so that you feel good when you hit the road.

Detailing the car is nice, but it's also time consuming. When I say to clean the car, I mean to make it feel fresh and welcoming so that you can fully relax and enjoy your road trip. This fresh-up includes shaking out floor mats, vacuuming the floors and seats, cleaning the cup holders, and cleaning the windows. In total, it will probably take less than an hour to freshen things up.

Cleaning the inside of your car before you leave really is worth it and you'll feel great about starting your trip.

Complete Gear Layout

The best way to evaluate if you're bringing necessities is to lay everything out and look at it as a big picture. I like to do this two or three days before a trip.

As you're going through your packing lists, get your gear, clothing, random supplies, and empty food containers you'll use (a bag, a bin, a cooler, etc.) and place them all together in a neat, easy-to-see fashion. Then stand back and look at it all.

"Do I actually need that?" and "I know I'm not going to wear all of these outfits . . ." start to run through your mind. Once you've given everything that second thought and you know you're only bringing what you need, you can start packing things.

Pack your clothing into duffel bags versus hard-sided suitcases. Pack gear that has a specific purpose for a specific activity together, such as hiking boots or beach gear. You can pack gear in durable bags or if it's all large, set it aside until it's time to pack into the car. Then group all the shoes and flip-flops, again, placing them in a sturdy bag (think reusable grocery bag).

Set all of this aside; you'll get to load the car soon.

Be Ready Early

If you're leaving on a Friday, aim to have things ready to go on Wednesday. This means that you've got your gear assembled, your laundry done, and your bags packed.

This also means that you've done your road trip grocery shopping or you're doing it today (Wednesday). Being ready for your travel two days early allows you time to take care of things you might have initially forgotten, and to clean your house so you return to a welcoming, stress-free atmosphere; and then, ultimately, being ready early allows you to relax before you take off.

Having a bit of extra time before you leave on a road trip really is helpful. And here's a surprise bonus that sometimes works out for the better: *you can leave early*. If you're all set and have the flexibility, being ready early means you can leave sooner.

Thoughtfully Pack Your Vehicle

Finally, we're ready to pack the car. As you follow the steps for loading up your vehicle you may need to adjust what you're bringing, but ideally loading the car should be a one-and-done situation.

To make things as easy as possible, line up your gear next to your car with the largest items first. I say to do the biggest stuff at the beginning versus doing the most important stuff first, because you've already evaluated everything and what you're bringing along is all important, required gear. You're not bringing excess junk.

Once you've got things organized by size at the car, you're ready to actually load it!

PACKING THE CAR: STEP-BY-STEP

The order of operations for packing the car is important, as this ensures that you're able to fit the most used, most essential items into the vehicle. Also, it's easier to fit small things later versus trying to reconfigure to fit larger items.

If you load your vehicle in this order, you should be able to successfully fit the necessities; you'll be able to access important items easily, and you can keep your car organized fairly well over the course of your trip.

Tip: Think of the back of your vehicle like a six-pack. Mentally split it into six segments (A–F) and you'll easily be able to conquer packing your car efficiently and effectively.

Pack Vehicle Necessities

Look at your group of the largest items. Here you'll see your roadside emergency kit, your clothing bags, and your food storage. I call these daily vehicle necessities because they are things you'll need every day or in case of an emergency.

First, place your roadside emergency kit to one side in the back of your car. This way it's accessible but not blocking things you're more likely to need. **Space F**

Second, place your food bin and/or cooler to the other side in the back. You may be able to put the food bin on top of the cooler if you need space later. **Space E**

Third, load clothing bags opposite from the cooler. Place them closer to the trunk door. **Space A + B**

By packing these necessities first, you'll ensure that they make it into the car and you'll also be able to place them where they'll be easily accessible when needed and nothing else will prevent you from getting to them since they are at the sides.

Load Road Trip Gear

This is where things might get a bit messy, but an easy way to avoid that is by packing smaller items (such as shoes, playing cards, or flashlights) in reusable grocery bags. This keeps things from loosely rolling about and is a great way to ensure you keep like items together.

First, place items that you know you will need for specific activities near the back of the car's storage space. This way it'll be out of the way until it's needed, but still easily accessible. This includes things like binoculars, hiking boots, backpacks, etc. **Space D**

The next items to load will be the gear you're likely to use daily, such as beach towels, a picnic blanket, photography gear, or toiletries (if you aren't packing them in your clothing bag). These are things you'll need daily in many cases, so being at the front keeps you from having to move everything else every day. **Space C**

Set Up Main Passenger Space

Now it's time to load the things that will be used during driving time, or whenever you stop for whatever reason. Here, we'll get kids' travel trays sorted, make sure that there are appropriate charging cables available, and store whatever activities or electronics our passengers need in easily accessible places.

The most important things to save space for are the small cooler and dry snack bag. These will be added to the passenger area just before leaving, so as you load up the rest of the passenger gear, keep in mind the size of the food storage you need to add.

Note: I also like to keep the small car vacuum in the passenger area when the vehicle has enough space for it. Especially on beach trips or when there are kids, this is extra helpful because, annoying as it may be, the small vacuum can be used while driving to suck up sand and spills.

When you get to setting up the front seat of the car, this is where you'll want to add back in some of the things you removed in the cleaning process. Be sure that your vehicle manual, the registration and insurance information, and your travel plan have all been placed in the glove box or console compartment. Chances are you won't need to refer to any of these documents, but should an emergency arise . . .

Complete the Loading!

It's time to go! You've planned, you've prepped, you've packed, and now it's time for the finishing touches.

Have everyone that's a part of the trip check out their space. Have them load up any small things they need to bring, including stuffies if there are kids. Anything that doesn't have a good spot to live during the road trip should be placed in the rear storage area, most likely in Space D.

Add your small cooler and snack bag, and you're all set!

Really, the key to remaining organized on a road trip is cleaning out the car a bit at the end of each day. That'll help you keep things in their place, will keep the car smelling good, and each day you'll be able to start with a fresh feeling, ready to explore.

CHAPTER 3

ROAD TRIP FOOD

WHEN YOU HIT the open road, long stretches of highway tend to inspire two things: singing John Denver really loudly and eating lots of snacks. The singing can be good for you, but the snacking not so much.

PLANNING SNACKS FOR THE ROAD

Driving on an empty stomach makes me hangry. Driving long distances with hangry kids makes me miserable. So, to combat the bad moods on a road trip, thoughtful food planning and packing is a focus a few days before we leave.

Sure, you could head out and then stop for snacks whenever you're hungry, but that'll waste time and open the door for making a lot of unhealthy snap decisions.

What's the benefit of actually planning out your road trip snacks? Truly, being prepared is one of the easiest ways to make any trip more fun and relaxing, and that goes for food too. In addition to saving time, money, and calories, beginning your travel with snacks on hand also will help in case of an emergency.

A snack emergency? Really? Yes, totally. Should you be stuck in traffic and majorly delayed, having the right snacks can help you and your passengers stay calm and fed.

While you probably can't prep enough fresh produce to last you on a ten-day road trip, you can at least set up snackage for the first four or five days. As you start to see your supplies dwindle, thoughtfully stop into a grocery store to refresh what's most popular if needed. You can force your trip mates to eat through what's left before adding new snacks, but freshening up and restocking the cooler is always appreciated.

HEALTHY SNACKS YOU CAN BUY

Not everyone has the time or the desire to spend the days leading up to their vacation in the kitchen. I wish I did, and for certain trips I do (or I force myself to find the time), but the reality is that many people need to make a grocery list that gets them on the road without the added stress of food prep.

To keep the on-demand food choices on the healthier side, make a grocery list at home and then thoughtfully shop two days before your trip. I say two days so that if you think of something you missed or if you need to get more of something else, you can easily make another jaunt to the store before your vacation actually starts.

These are my top picks for road trip snacks that are on the healthier side, are easy to manage, and don't ruin easily:

- apples/grapes/blueberries
- baby carrots
- celery sticks
- meat sticks (healthy cured option—turkey or beef)
- pretzel rods (less messy than twists/sticks)
- trail mix
- mixed nuts
- freeze dried or regular dried fruit
- chewy/chunky granola bars
- cheese sticks or slices

While it may be difficult to convince your family that a combination of these different snacks could be considered a replacement for a meal, in a pinch or emergency you'll be so glad to have these items on hand.

HEALTHY SNACKS
YOU CAN MAKE AT HOME

Just like you can buy premade snacks of all sorts, you can also make them yourself before you hit the road. You'll actually save a bit of money, and by not generating a lot of plastic waste with all the wrappers, you'll be doing something good for the planet.

Healthy road trip snacks you can make at home range from prepping fresh produce to actually baking. You know what your strong suits are, and you know if baking a bunch before you leave is going to stress you out or not, so make the choice that is right for you.

But, if you do choose to make your own snacks, these options are great, easy, and much healthier than what you'll get at the store, and your road trip mates will appreciate the time and care you've put into thinking about them before the trip.

As you start to prep your road snacks, consider reusable containers for them, such as stackable sandwich containers. Zippered bags are also good and are easy to pack in a cooler.

- apple or pear slices
- carrot or celery sticks
- cucumber sticks or rounds
- cheese slices
- deli rolled meats/quality deli cuts*
- morning glory muffins (bran)

- snack mix*
- roasted seasoned nuts*
- breakfast cookies
- dried fruit*

* Recipe follows.

To add some substance to fresh produce snacks, have cream cheese or peanut butter (or another alternative) ready for dipping. You may have to manage that process a bit more if you've got small kids in the car, but it brings variety to the snacks and will keep tummies happier longer.

For the morning glory muffins and breakfast cookies noted in the DIY snack list, these items can vary greatly and it's best to attempt these long before your road trip. You'll want to use a recipe that has ingredients you like and that stays moist for several days. I use oat flour and raisins in mine, which does the trick, but you can find a new recipe each time to keep things interesting.

Keeping Snacks Fresh

To keep your snacks fresh, properly storing them is key. Yes, you need to keep produce cold. No, you can't smash cookies and muffins and expect a clean car.

To keep produce fresh on your road trip, be sure to use a small cooler in your vehicle. If you have the space to bring a large cooler, like you would for a camping trip, that's great, but if not, a small cooler, even a soft-sided cooler, should do the trick.

I love our electric cooler that plugs into our twelve-volt outlet in the car. At night, we bring it into our hotel room and use the plug converter to maintain its temperature until we're back on the road.

For sliced/prepared produce, there are some wonderful natural solutions for keeping them fresh and crisp (in addition to keeping them cold). For apples, pears, grapes, blueberries, or strawberries, add a hearty squeeze of lemon to them after they are prepped. This will keep them from oxidizing and will maintain their overall freshness longer. For cucumber sticks or slices, a bit of lime juice and a few mint leaves will keep them snappy . . . and then you'll have the perfect mojito fixings for later.

If you're bringing carrot or jicama sticks, a little water, a dash of salt, and a well-sealed container should do the trick to maintain their freshness. With jicama, check out the recipe below for a fun, delicious way to make a boring healthy snack more appealing.

RECIPES FOR DIY HEALTHY SNACKS

Hooray! You're creating some delicious, unique snacks to enjoy on your road trip and guess what . . . You're making them healthier than what you'd normally get at the store! DIY healthy road trip snacks are a great use of your pre-trip time, and once you've tried it, you'll do it for every trip.

As with any recipe, always feel empowered to adjust to your own tastes and needs. Also, make sure to consider any allergies your travel group might have. Happy snacking!

Deli Meat Roll-ups

This may sound weird at first, but this snack is hearty, delicious, and holds well over several days. The small amount of prep that goes into these really makes the first few days of a road trip easy to tackle.

Ingredients: deli meat, cream cheese or hummus, crunchy vegetables

1. Choose your deli meat, medium sliced
2. Spread cream cheese OR hummus thinly across meat slice
3. Place crunchy vegetable on spread
4. Roll up and stack in container

So easy. So delicious.

For the deli meat roll-ups, you can use a variety of crunchy vegetables when you make them. My favorite is pickled asparagus, but cornichons, half-width celery sticks, thinly sliced carrots, or even English cucumber sticks are a good addition.

When you're purchasing the deli meat, there are several good options: smoked turkey, ham, salami, Lebanon bologna, or even prosciutto.

Vegetarian options include products like Tofurky or seitan. If you just want to turn the roll-ups into small wraps, tortillas can easily be substituted for the meat, just be cautious of how moist they may get depending on your filling.

Healthy bonus: Celery and hummus are the two most health-conscious fillers, and both stay fresh for quite a while.

Seasoned Nuts

A lot of people have nut allergies or intolerances, so walk this path with caution. A great thing about making your own seasoned nut mix for road trips is that you're in complete control of what goes into it, including the types of nuts. I personally am allergic to almonds so I avoid them at all costs, but somebody else in your crew may be allergic to peanuts.

As you make this recipe, adjust it based on likes/dislikes, allergens, and the reality of how many people are actually going to be eating it. A great thing about making too much of a seasoned nut mix is that it will keep for a long time. This recipe makes three to four cups or one quart-size bag/container.

Ingredients: raw or roasted whole nuts (pecans, almonds, cashews, etc.), kosher salt, 2 tbsp olive or avocado oil, black pepper, crushed red pepper, dried basil, onion powder

1. Preheat oven to 300 degrees F
2. Sort through the nuts to be sure there are no shells remaining
3. Warm the oil in a small skillet on the stove, but don't let it smoke
4. Mix your seasonings into the oil: 1 tsp crushed red pepper, 1 tsp black pepper, 2 tsp dried basil, 1 tsp onion powder

5. Add the warm seasoned oil to the bowl of shell-free nuts and stir, stir, stir!

6. Stir in 1 tbsp of kosher salt. OPTIONAL: Sprinkle a tsp of sugar also. Skip this to keep the nuts healthier and prevent sticky fingers.

7. Evenly place seasoned nuts on a lipped baking sheet

8. Bake for fifteen minutes, rotating the nuts occasionally

Once the nuts cool, place them in a container or zippered bag to enjoy on your road trip!

If you aren't a fan of spice, that's okay. Replace the red pepper flakes with paprika and add a dash of liquid smoke during the mixing process. You can also add dashes of cumin, garlic powder, or oregano to change it up and make different flavor profiles.

Road Trip Snack Mix

Snack mix. It's my downfall, but I still make it and share it. Okay, I don't share it.

Depending on where you're from, you'll have a different idea of what makes a good snack mix. For some it means you mix cheesy crackers with croutons and nuts, and for others it just means there are pretzels in a bag with literally anything else.

For me and my family, snack mix is all about crunch, balance, and flavor. As you make your own snack mix, choose the crackers and crunches that you like best, or are what you'd consider the healthiest.

Mix suggestions: cheese crackers, bagel crisps, small croutons, rye crisps, pretzel sticks or twists, pita chips, cashews or peanuts

Ingredients for seasoning: garlic powder, onion powder, oregano, marjoram (optional), 2 tbsp butter

1. Preheat oven to 300 degrees F
2. In a bowl, toss together your crunchy mix, monitoring how much you're making in total
3. Melt the butter (melt a little extra if you're doing a large batch)
4. Mix your seasonings into the butter: 1 tsp dried oregano, 1 tsp garlic powder, 1 tsp onion powder, 1 tsp marjoram (optional for a hearty flavor); add salt if you think it's needed
5. Add the warm seasoned butter to your crunchy mix and stir, stir, stir!
6. Evenly place seasoned mix on a lipped baking sheet (or two)
7. Bake for fifteen minutes, stirring/turning occasionally

Once the mix cools, move to large zippered bags or containers.

There are lots of varieties of snack mix you can create. Sweet and salty is another great one and it's easy to do. Just use a mix of plain-flavored crackers, including a cheesy one, and leave out the spices. Add 2 tsp of sugar when you mix it, and it will be just a bit sweet and the tiniest bit caramelized after it's baked.

You'll love these great road trip snack mixes!

DIY Dried Fruit

For some people dried fruit is a treat and for others it's a last resort. For my family it's right in between.

When making your own dried fruit, there are two approaches: natural or bonus sweetness. Since I'm all about doing things a bit healthier than what you can typically get in the grocery store, let's start with natural-style dried fruit.

The best types of fruit to dry, meaning that they tend to turn out the best in terms of texture and flavor, are apples, peaches, and pears. You can also dry strawberries, kiwis, and blueberries, but they tend to turn out much more crispy or hard to chew, and kiwi can turn bitter.

When preparing fruit to be dehydrated, you'll want to cut it to be thick enough to retain a soft center, but thin enough that it will genuinely dry out, leaving minimal moisture in the individual pieces. In general, with almost every type of fruit you might dry, slices just under ¼" thick should be ideal.

If you're drying berries, whether they be blueberries or strawberries, leave them whole for the drying process, just removing any greenery. For larger strawberries, cut them in half, but still leave them pretty thick.

The actual drying process may vary. My grandma used to hang fruit on a line or place it in the oven at a very low temperature for a long time.

I like to use a food dehydrator with a fan in it, but that's because I'm impatient. Getting a food dehydrator that's expandable, meaning it has many racks, is a great way to dry a lot of fruit all at once. The more racks, the slower the process, but also the softer the fruit.

Something to note with drying fruit is that as it dries, it shrinks. While you might think that one apple, a pear, and ten strawberries is a lot of fruit, once dried it really isn't very much. If you want to make enough road trip snacks to last through your trip, consider drying one fresh fruit serving per person per day. That may seem like a ton, but when it's dried and your traveling crew is snacking, you'll see how quickly it goes.

The following chart will help you decide how much fruit to buy for drying, assuming not everybody will like each type of fruit or there may be a few allergies.

Ingredients:
Slice fruit to desired thickness, up to ¼" thick

1. Prepare drying rack by lightly coating with nonstick spray
2. Distribute sliced fruit evenly across the racks, allowing small spaces between pieces for air to flow through
3. Turn on dehydrator and place racks on it
4. Monitor drying process, rotating the racks to allow all fruit to dehydrate evenly

5. As fruit dries, remove pieces that have reached desired dehydration; the longer on the racks, the crispier the fruit
6. Keep the dried fruit in an airtight container or freezer bag. Be sure that you shake it once a day to keep the fruit from sticking together

Note: If you're using an oven to dry fruit, setting it to 225 degrees F is a good temperature to ensure you're not cooking the fruit, but just drying it. If you have a convection feature, turn it on and lower the temp a bit. Just as with the dehydrator, the fruit will be well shriveled when it's ready.

Another way to prepare dried fruit as a healthy road trip snack, and this only makes it a little sweeter but in a natural way, is to soak the fruit in juice before dehydrating. Soaking it in apple juice will make it sweeter (and add sugar), or you can soak it in pineapple juice, which both sweetens it up and helps to preserve its color instead of turning brown.

If you want to preserve the color but not add a bunch of sugar, just soak your fruit in warm water with lemon juice before you dehydrate it. The acid in the lemon or pineapple juice helps to both kill bacteria and keep the fruit from oxidizing (browning).

Tales from the Road: Dried fruit can be really easy to just snack away at, especially something like apple chips. Too much dried fruit can also do a number on the stomach, though. Our youngest loves it, every kind. On a road trip out of San Francisco, we were having a long day in the car and he was having a long snacking session on dried blueberries and strawberries. Suddenly, a panic came from the back seat and we pulled over on the highway really quickly.

As soon as we got him out of the car, he had to drop his pants and relieve himself of the massive amount of fruit he'd been enjoying. It was pretty bad, and he was really upset. We had to do this several more times that day. Now we're much more cautious about providing dried fruit on road trips.

Besides making all these wonderful snacks for a road trip, you can make them and keep them on hand just for everyday life too. Enjoy!

PLANNING MEALS FOR YOUR ROAD TRIP

Food is an adventure all its own. I'm not going to glamorize the world of highway takeout or make it seem like an Instagram-worthy picnic is super easy, but road trip meals can be awesome and memorable.

I know that in our house, we're big into picnicking. I even write about it as its own subject matter for websites about destinations and travel. If it's not your jam, that's fine, but here you'll find some pretty solid tips and tricks to up your road trip picnic game.

Also, about that highway takeout I mentioned, there are actually some pretty iconic roadside diners you might discover, and with the growth of the food truck industry, gourmet discoveries are easier than ever.

Depending on your travel style and budget, you may be planning on being your own chef for the majority of your road trip meals, and that's absolutely fine. But be prepared for a variety of dining scenarios and environments if that's your plan, because road trip life can be a mixed bag, for sure. Here's how you plan and pack for great meals on your road trip.

DIY HIGHWAY LUNCHES

I'm all about enjoying the stops along the way, adding a short hike if time allows, and making sure my travel team is fed and happy. With that, being ready to prep a quick meal or snack is key to road trip success. DIY highway lunches sometimes don't happen as often as we plan, and sometimes the plan is just thrown out the window and we live out our best picnic dreams.

Finding the Right Place to Picnic

Safety is always at the forefront of my mind when I'm traveling. On road trips, safety is even more paramount as there are so many things that can go wrong. Don't let pulling off your route for a picnic be one of them.

As you plan out your stops for meals, there are lots of things to consider:

- atmosphere
- shelter
- ease of access
- bathrooms

→ Picnic Atmosphere

Is your perfect picnic location just on the side of the road, or do you want a lunch with a view? Since mealtimes can be difficult to predict on a road trip, finding the right atmosphere can be tricky. If enjoying a view or having an activity to go along with your meal stop is important, planning picnic stops should be done in advance.

With map technology being so well updated today and with users adding photos through apps and search services, researching picnic spots is easier than ever.

"So how do I find a picnic spot?"

In the earlier planning section, Researching Destinations and Attractions, I talked about leveraging travel blogs and user-created information to find great stops along your road trip route, and this includes picnic spots. Apps like AllTrails and Google Maps include recent photos from those who've visited, and actual reviews of certain types of sites. Use this information!

To find a picnic spot, in general, you can also just seek out rest areas or state parks. You'll find the best road trip picnic atmosphere within the parks and away from the interstate, but if you need to keep on schedule and don't want to stray too far, rest areas tend to have picnic tables and green space to stretch your legs and have lunch.

Tip: Don't underestimate the beauty of local parks. National and state parks are known for having incredible sights, but in many areas local (county or city) parks are also home to remarkable picnic areas. Examples: Shoshone Falls in Twin Falls, ID, or Gemini Springs in DeBary, FL. Both are local, just off the highway, and have phenomenal natural wonders.

→ Shelter for Any Weather

Weather is something we're just not in control of. No matter how much we hope and plan, weather can sometimes get the best of us. When we're planning our road trip picnic stops, we are careful to look for options that have both designated picnic shelters and open space.

Taking a break from being in the car to enjoy a meal can be refreshing, and if you can get some sunshine while you're doing it, that's a bonus. Depending on where you are and the time of year, that same sunshine might be a bit intense, in which case a picnic shelter is nice to have, both for hot sun or unexpected rain.

The best way to research picnic area shelters in advance is to look at online user images of the locations you're considering. Yes, local websites may provide information about the types of picnicking available, but user images can give a fuller picture of what to expect, including the number of shelters.

Should you choose to do a roadside picnic NOT at a designated picnic area, just remember to always pack out what you pack in and leave no trace that you were there.

→ Ease of Access

I can't tell you how many times I've pulled off the freeway and not realized that there wasn't an on-ramp back onto the road. Yes, I've learned the hard way about that one.

Whether you're finding a picnic spot on the fly or you're actually planning it out, take a moment to consider how far off course your stop will take you. If you're fine adding some travel time, great! But if staying on schedule is important to you, be sure that you can quickly get back on track after your picnic lunch.

I like to keep lunch sites within ten minutes of our travel route. This way it's usually quiet enough to really enjoy the nature around us, but also not so inconvenient that we're stuck in local traffic just to get back to the highway.

→ Bathrooms and Other Services

Yes, bathrooms are important. While using the facilities is a very normal, human thing to do, a lot of people have anxiety about using public restrooms for many reasons. As you plan your picnic stops, consider whether or not there are restrooms or other services that you and your crew can take advantage of.

There's a lot to be said for nice convenience stops along a road trip route. Washing hands and freshening up is important and keeps the energy level high, so finding picnic stops that can offer this is smart, thoughtful planning.

Five Ways to Do Meals in the Car

There really are lots of ways to plan your road trip meals, specifically midday/lunches. If you've developed an awesome itinerary that you really need to stick to, great, do it; but if you have some flexibility, mix it up over the course of your trip. Having sandwich or wrap makings in your cooler will set you up for success each morning of your adventure.

And don't worry, we'll get to roadside restaurants soon . . .

→ Prepacking Lunches

For the planner or the family that has a lot of ground to cover, or for the hikers or the beach bums, prepacking lunches is a great way to ensure your crew stays happy no matter where you find yourselves.

Try making a little sandwich assembly line before you leave your hotel for the day. To keep it easy, I don't usually let my family have any say in what I make when the time comes, but I've already got sandwich supplies they like, so there's no worries when it's actually time to eat.

When prepacking lunches, stacking bagels or sliced bread sandwiches is an easy way to make a transportable lunch kit. I like to have a dedicated hard-sided container that fits four sandwiches, but a simple bread bag (from your sandwich bread) will do as well.

And don't forget, you already have fruit and veggies to accompany your lunch on the go, so just making sandwiches or wraps in the morning is all you need to worry about.

→ Al Fresco Dining and Gear

Yes, I always feel like a picnic or dining al fresco is a paradise-type experience . . . unless we stop somewhere that has lots of flies or mosquitoes. But let's just pretend that never happens.

For a perfect picnic during a road trip, you can either prepack lunches (as mentioned above) or you can treat the great outdoors like your own kitchen and make your meal al fresco. Taking this approach requires a bit more planning and equipment.

For the perfect picnic in paradise, plan to pack the following before you ever hit the road:

- picnic blanket or large sheet
- outdoor tablecloth
- cutting board
- reusable cutlery
- reusable plates
- sandwich supplies (mayo, mustard, etc.)

Again, a little planning goes a long way. Being ready to take advantage of the beautiful outdoors makes any road trip experience memorable and something you'll talk about for years to come. Be sure to check out the Best Road Trip Picnic Menus section later in this chapter for my favorite things to make when outdoor dining.

And since I mentioned it just a moment ago, yes, there can be bugs flying about during a picnic. If you're in an area where this may be a problem (think moist air, near a stream or meadow), using a bit of natural insect repellent is very helpful. We gravitate toward the products that have lemongrass and eucalyptus oils in them vs. DEET. Going natural is ideal in general, and when you're picnicking, if you don't have a handwashing station immediately available, natural repellents are a good safety precaution.

→ Snack Smorgasbord

My kids love when we just have never-ending snacks instead of meals, but I personally need to keep that bit of structure in my life, especially when we're on the road. That said, this doesn't mean it's not right for others. Leveraging your well-thought-out snacks can work just fine on some road trip days.

I strongly recommend *deciding* to have a snack meal on your schedule versus being forced into the situation. It's just better for moods and I always like to set expectations for the day when road trips include people that I know get hangry.

If you want to make the snack smorgasbord extra fun, shop for a unique dessert or beverage to go along with snack meals. For example, the night before when you're walking around whatever town you're at, grab some locally made cookies or artisan sodas. Regional snacks can really vary all across North America, so take advantage of it!

→ Unplanned Dining Finds

Food trucks. Farmers markets. Dairy freeze stands. There are so many wonderful places that pepper the highways and small towns while road-tripping. While it's not a guarantee that every stretch of road is going to have the perfect slice of local eats, if you keep your eyes peeled, no doubt you'll find something good each day.

To allow room for these awesome unplanned dining finds, when you're setting up your daily driving route, do a quick online search using a map tool (such as Google Maps) to zoom into the area around your path. Search with terms like "stand" or "food truck" or even "village." These terms are commonly associated with movable or mom-n-pop–style food choices.

If you're doing a road trip from spring through fall, let yourself be drawn to farmers' markets or festivals. I love when we visit a new place and get to support the small, local businesses face-to-face, and farmers' markets are one of the best ways to do that. And what's really great is that farmers' markets are specific to any one region but are common in small towns and large cities alike all across the US and Canada.

So many wonderful opportunities to stumble upon great food!

→ Get It to Go

Getting lunch to go and eating in the car is by far my least favorite dining option when I'm on the road, but sometimes it's necessary. This doesn't mean we're getting lunch at a fast-food chain and stinking up the car like old grease, but that *sometimes* happens. What I'm talking about is thoughtfully finding food that you'll enjoy *and* that you can easily eat in the car.

Recent years have seen incredible changes to how restaurants operate, including making their dining options mobile. While one person is driving, another could be doing some research on their phone to find a great place with lots of good reviews, then ordering ahead and quickly stopping to pick it up. Ordering to-go may not be ideal, but it'll work if you can't dedicate time to sitting in a restaurant or are tired of snack meals.

Open your mind to the many possibilities that are available by ordering lunch to go.

Best Road Trip Picnic Menus

Hooray! This is my favorite part of road trip meals: amazing picnic spreads out in nature!

All of these menu options can be created in the morning before you hit the road. All you'll need to do is a little shopping, either before your road trip or the night before your planned picnic.

→ Fancy Sandwich Spread

I may be raising my kids to be sandwich snobs. It's too early to tell, but this is their favorite picnic meal. Yes, in normal life we eat a lot of sandwiches (and not just at lunch), but picnic sandwiches for some reason are extra special.

Yes, there are trips where my sandwiching skills cap out at PB&J, but when I've been thoughtful about it and allow myself time during the trip, I have created some wonderful meals. To make a sandwich-based picnic a bit fancier, use a few ingredients that you wouldn't normally use at home. And have crisp, cold pickles at the ready, just like a real, picture-perfect delicatessen would.

The following is our family's favorite sandwich: the Seven-Layer Sandy.

INGREDIENTS:

- rustic or normal bread
- mayonnaise
- stone ground mustard
- fig jam
- thin-sliced turkey and ham
- sliced cheese (cheddar is best)
- pickled onions
- cucumber
- alfalfa sprouts

How to:

Spread the mayo and mustard on the bread, followed by a turkey slice or two. Add a thin spread of fig jam to the turkey, then add a slice of cheese. A layer of alfalfa sprouts (not too much) topped with a few thin slices of cucumber brings a whole lot of freshness to the stack. One more slice of cheese, some ham, and close that sandwich up.

Alternatives to mayo and mustard include hummus and guacamole, which both make delicious and healthier sandwiches.

→ Cheese and Charcuterie in a Meadow

What? You don't know the term *charcuterie*? Charcuterie refers to the curing and preserving of meats. Often these wonderful meats, such as speck and salami, are served with cheeses, nuts, and fruit products. At home, charcuterie is my downfall. I eat all the things in one sitting . . .

On a road trip, planning a charcuterie meal is just as exciting, if not more so because you will be enjoying it in the great outdoors. And it's extremely easy; it doesn't have to be presented all fancy if you don't want to, but you could.

The following ingredients are suggestions to pick from, but you know what you like and what your family will enjoy. If something from the list isn't available, substitute anything else. That's why this option is so easy and delicious!

FLEXIBLE INGREDIENTS (CHEESE IN CHUNKS AND MEAT IN SLICES):

- gruyere cheese
- blue or gorgonzola crumbles
- brie or camembert cheese
- cheddar (an Irish cheddar is best)
- salami (Genoa or hard)
- speck ham
- prosciutto
- landjäger (a European sausage that can be kept at room temperature)

- dried fruit
- smoked nuts
- variety of crackers
- crusty bread
- fig jam

How to:

On plates or cutting boards arrange your meats together and then cheeses opposite. Between them, add one type of cracker or crusty bread. On another plate or board, place your dried fruits, remaining meats and cheeses, jam, or anything else you want to include.

Even though this seems like such a free-for-all meal (or maybe more like a cocktail party setup), this is a great picnic option that is filling, fun, and fancier than you thought possible to go along with a road trip.

→ Wraps and Pinwheels

Much like making fancy sandwiches, wraps and pinwheels are a big hit with kids. I love mixing up our road trip meals by adding a wrap day because it doesn't take terribly different ingredients than sandwiches but feels like a very different meal.

Also, wraps often travel better than multilayered sandwiches. When it comes to making wraps for road trip picnics, I like to really work in the vegetables. Building a lunch wrap like you would a burrito, you can fill it with whatever goodness your heart desires, just as long as you can successfully close it.

INGREDIENTS:

- tortillas/wraps
- cream cheese/hummus/guacamole
- thin-sliced lunch meats
- thin-sliced cheese
- red bell pepper slices

- alfalfa sprouts
- cucumber spears

How to wrap: Just as with sandwiches, start by spreading your binding ingredient (cream cheese, guac, or hummus) over most of the tortilla surface. Make a stack of other ingredients longways in the center. Fold the tortilla over the two ends of the filling stack, then tightly roll from left to right, keeping the first folds tucked in. If you've spread the cream cheese (or whatever you choose) nearly to the edge, your wrap should hold itself together nicely.

How to pinwheel: When it comes to making pinwheels, you have to have a slightly more skilled approach and you need to use larger tortillas or wraps. To make pinwheels, follow the same steps above, but spread the filling ingredients out versus making a stack. When you roll it, you don't need to tuck the ends in first, but still roll it tightly. Slice the roll into four or five pieces, making nice lunch pinwheels that can quell any appetite.

When packing up your lunch, since tortillas and wraps tend to stick together when then get moist, separate them with a paper towel, napkin, or foil if you have it. For pinwheels, they're best transported in a hard container.

→ Fine Deli Dining

Does that sound ironic? "Fine deli dining" . . . I know that might seem like the opposite of fine dining but getting everything you need for a nice picnic during your road trip is as easy as stopping at a local deli and getting a selection of salads and such.

While it's always nice to find a small, local deli with unique options and secret recipes for all of their menu items, grocery store deli counters tend to have a great variety of choices too. I like planning a deli lunch day because it takes the extra task of preparing lunch off my plate.

Another bonus to scheduling a deli lunch day is that you can special-order fancy sandwiches in addition to picking up macaroni salad and coleslaw. With little effort, you can put together a stellar picnic by spending ten minutes at the deli counter.

My family's favorite deli options include:

- macaroni salad
- pasta salad
- potato salad
- creamy coleslaw
- kale slaw
- pea salad
- po'boys (French roll sandwich)
- custom turkey sandwiches

I love finding local delis when we're on a road trip. I especially love trying EVERY type of coleslaw, as they vary so much by region.

An added bonus to doing a deli picnic is that you can also add a charcuterie element to your outdoor luncheon. Between a bit of cured meat and maybe a selection from the olive bar (my other favorite), you can put together a movable feast.

Green Tips for Food on the Road

Food production and consumption in general creates a lot of waste. When you're on a road trip, it's very easy to add to that, particularly when it comes to snacks and prewrapped foods. Also, even though every day more businesses change their operations to be greener, there are still pockets of North America where you'll find Styrofoam and plastic straws.

There's more to it than that, though. Green choices when it comes to food and dining during road trips start before you ever leave the house. Here are ten ways you can maximize your greenness while on the road:

1. Prepare your own road trip snacks and meals
2. Pack snacks in reusable containers

3. Bring reusable cutlery, including your own metal straws
4. Use metal water bottles and refill them often
5. Reusable coffee cups and tumblers are better than disposable ones
6. Dine in when you can (no carry-out waste)
7. Eat or shop as local as possible
8. Bring your own bags or growlers (if you plan to purchase locally brewed beer on your trip)
9. Decline excess serve ware, condiments, or to-go supplies
10. Opt for fruit and vegetable snacks that *are* their own packaging

Small steps and actions, when taken by many, have a big impact. Being thoughtful about your consumption during a road trip and sharing that with others will have a lasting effect on the places you visit.

DINING OUT ON YOUR ROUTE

One of my favorite road trip themes is having a foodie experience. You can learn so much about an area's culture by digging into their food. This might be white linen dining or even grabbing tacos from a converted school bus restaurant. There are so many experiences just waiting for you!

But the other side of this is that road trips are considered to be one of the most budget-friendly types of vacations, and the cost of dining out adds up very quickly. How can you balance having exceptional dining experiences with sticking to a budget? So glad you asked.

Since so much of my road trip travel is work related, I come with a built-in budget, a per diem if you will. Since I often have to bill back dining expenses and have lots of practice with that, I apply those same principles to how my family manages food costs on our own vacations.

Creating a Dining Out Budget for Your Road Trip

Yes, budgets are important in so many parts of life, and road trips definitely warrant budgeting as well. I'm not going to dive deeply into annual budgeting or even overall vacation budgeting, just how you can project and plan for the costs of dining out on the road.

Building a Realistic Daily Dining Budget

When we build our daily budget, we follow a simple formula: one dine out per day, two budget prepped meals per day.

MEAL OUT	ADULT X2	CHILD X2	TOTAL	
BREAKFAST	12	7	38	WE CHOOSE THESE OPTIONS
LUNCH	14	7	42	
DINNER	22	8	60	TOTAL PROJECTED COST, AT THE LOW END: $100 PER DAY

MEAL PREPPED*	ADULT X2	CHILD X2	TOTAL
BREAKFAST	4	4	16
LUNCH	6	6	24
DINNER	7	6	26

* Estimates based on shared ingredients, overestimated; projected costs in USD.

The numbers above are all estimates based on costs I've documented on a variety of trips. When you're prepping meals, you share ingredients, so the costs stay low.

Note: This budget is extremely on point with our daily spending for our own road trips. If you factor in experiences like brewery tours or dessert stops, it goes up, but in general, our family of four costs around $100 per day to feed on the road. Be honest with yourself, though, and if you think you need to budget for dining out more, do it.

We know that some days we won't spend anything on breakfast because we've already brought breakfast cookies or muffins and fruit, but then other days we may do a quick coffee shop stop. We also know that we make a lot of our lunches because we do a lot of picnics, hikes, or beach days, so that's going to save us money. And finally, we know there's zero chance of our making our own dinner during a road trip, unless the weather is amazing and we have access to a barbecue.

Because we're big on picnics in our family, we are able to set a lower food budget than you might expect. Making our own meal at least once a day saves us quite a bit of money when you look at the big picture. And on some days we'll make both breakfast and lunch ourselves (or breakfast might be provided at our hotel).

Tips for a Smaller Road Trip Food Spend

Whether you plan on making some of your road trip meals or not, you always have the ability to choose how much you're spending on your meals. With rare exception, the style of dining you choose will 100 percent be reflected in what you spend each day. If you're eating steak and lobster for every meal, your wallet will feel it.

Here are some things to consider in order to keep dining expenditures on the lower end:

- Cost of supplies for four gourmet DIY sandwiches: about $12–$15 USD

- Cost of four lunch menu meals at a midgrade restaurant: $36–$60 USD
- A nice but not fancy, locally owned restaurant dinner for four (2A, 2K): $45–$70 USD
- Upscale dining with a nice view for four (2A, 2K): $65–$90 USD

Making choices that favor sticking to your budget before it's mealtime will help you both plan your days and spend less in the long run.

Tip: While it's nice to enjoy a beer or glass of wine while dining out, you can decide to hold off and get a bottle of wine from the store to share back at your hotel. Even if you choose a nice bottle, you'll no doubt save around 70 percent over the cost of ordering in the restaurant.

Planning Exceptional Dining Experiences

Research, whether a month in advance or the hour before you pull off the freeway, is very helpful for finding the best dining options for your travel crew, both to find food everyone will enjoy and to not have to wait a long time if you choose a popular place (you can call ahead). And research will also help you stick with your dining budget while traveling.

I love going someplace new and learning that they have regional specialties. For example, did you know that the St. Augustine area of Florida actually has a deep history of Minorcan culture due to indentured servants coming to America long ago?[1] This means there are local flavors, like the datil pepper, that you won't find anywhere else. And that means Minorcan chowder is on the menu too!

Because we take the time to research food, we learn about these great, unique elements and seek out dining experiences that include them. Just because we're researching restaurants and meal ideas in advance doesn't mean we're looking for the most exclusive or expensive options, just finding the must-try items that characterize the area.

To make the most of dining out on your road trip:

- research to find history in the food
- read beyond page one of search results for dining options
- ask a local for a dish and dining recommendations
- stop when you see a food stand with a hand-painted sign
- never underestimate the power of a food truck

A little research goes a long way. And as you find foods that you've just got to try, spy on the internet for menus so you can estimate prices. I'm always looking to stay within my budget, even when it comes to must-try dining on the road.

FOOD STORAGE IN THE CAR

Staying organized helps to maintain calm in many aspects of road-tripping. Organizing personal space, organizing time, organizing the trunk, and organizing food and snacks are all ways to manage stress and keep things mellow. It's important that things be in their place, but also easy to get to.

I love packing the car before a trip and then leading my family through orientation. I'm a dork like that, but I think that's also why we have such wonderful trips together. There are many ways to align expectations, and how and where food is stored is actually more important than you might think.

Imagine hitting the road and your front-seat passenger starts digging around in the dry snack bag and unknowingly spills the seasoned garlic nuts all over the floor . . . and then still doesn't find the snack they wanted. *Boom*. You've created an exceptional mess *and* your vehicle is going to smell bad for the next ten days.

FOOD ORGANIZATION FOR A ROAD TRIP

Yes, having a good organization plan for your food during a road trip is just as important as making sure you packed underwear and socks. Having a good system and keeping things in order will help your travel group stay well supplied with snacks, and you'll actually eat the food you bring.

Dry Food Storage in the Car

I love that we have a larger vehicle for road trips because it means we don't have to skimp on how we use the space. I like to have a snack bag in the passenger area or front seat and then a hard-sided box or storage bin in the back as well. In the bag, which is the most accessible food storage space, we'll keep prepared snacks like dried fruit, granola bars, or snack mix.

We'll store the more crushable items, meaning crackers, chips, or bread in a box or small bin in the back or trunk of the vehicle. It's important to have the two separate storage spaces so that items don't get destroyed, and to pace everyone so all the snacks don't disappear in one leg of the road trip.

Tip: If you're limited on space, work with what you've got and accept that at some point you'll need to get more snacks. I always prefer to be fully loaded and snack-ready at the start of the trip, but to save space and to not smash delicate foods, shop as needed along the way.

Coolers and Cold Food

Cold food, like intentionally cold food, is such a welcome refreshment on a road trip. Your family or travel buddies will think you're so well prepared if you offer them a chilled snack or cold soda as you drive through the desert.

In our family we do road trips with two coolers: a small one up front and a large one in the rear storage area.

In the small one we keep snacks like carrots, apples, and maybe some fizzy waters. In the larger cooler we store our lunch fixings and backup snacks.

Because we do so many picnic lunches and breakfasts on the go, the large cooler is very important to us. We do a substantial grocery shop before we leave on a road trip, and this is mostly kept in the large cooler. It's wonderful to have your own supplies and dietary needs close at hand.

Note: The small cooler we use on trips departing from our own driveway is a twelve-volt iceless cooler. It's great for keeping things cold, it's compact, and we can plug it in in our hotel room at night.

On trips where we've flown to the starting point of our road trip, we still bring a small, soft cooler with us. With this flying type of road trip, we do less of our own meal prep and more of the to-go or deli-style lunches.

It's important to find your own groove for bringing food on a trip. If the meal prep and cooler system doesn't fit with your style or vehicle type, so be it. Do what works for *you*.

Beware of Heat

Cars can sometimes act like ovens. When you're traveling with food, be sure you're taking rising temperatures into consideration. When the interior temperature reaches over 130 degrees (which is what happens on a typical 80-degree day), cooler ice melts faster and food that isn't stored in a cooler can go bad or stale very quickly.

There are ways to help minimize that interior temperature, though:

- park in shady areas or parking garages
- use reflective window and windshield screens
- allow air circulation even when parked by opening a sunroof or window a bit
- travel only in the winter (I'm kidding)

Case in point: If you don't manage how hot your vehicle can get, you may waste a lot of money when your road trip food goes bad.

CLEANLINESS AND EATING IN THE CAR

You can't do a road trip without some form of eating in the car, whether that's snacking or actual meals. You can try, but it's highly unlikely that you'll make it past day one without eating in your vehicle. Best to be prepared to keep the mess to a minimum!

In-Car Cleaning Supplies

There are many wonderful, portable cleaning products you can keep on hand for road trips. The easiest supplies to get a hold of seem to be napkins from random drive-thrus, but you can be intentional with your in-car cleaning supplies too.

Baby wipes are really incredible for keeping grubby hands clean (and faces too). While I don't recommend them for detailing your seats and dash, they are ideal for fixing up messy humans.

Sanitizing wipes, such as Lysol products, are wonderful as well. While not recommended for cleaning little kids' faces, they do an amazing job at destickifying vehicle interior surfaces. Particularly as travelers are making efforts to sanitize more often, wipes that contain antibacterial agents are great to keep in the car.

Hopefully you won't be spilling any beverages on your next road trip, but just in case you do, have a roll or two of paper towels on hand. To make them go a bit further and to ensure they're as absorbent as possible, it's okay to spend a few extra dollars to get *good* paper towels. You have permission to get what you need. You'll thank me later.

Lastly, trash receptacles are a must. It's very helpful in keeping things tidy if you have two designated trash bags or bins in your car. I'm sure to have one in the front seat, one in the middle (in our three-row vehicle), and one in the back. It doesn't hurt to keep a few extra bags on hand as well, particularly if you're picnicking and need to pack out your trash.

Managing Accumulated Mess

In the earlier section Versatile Road Trip Gear, I mention having a small vacuum in the car. Yes, it's actually needed. Even if you're not doing a beach-based vacation, you'll be continually tracking in dirt and sand. And even if you're not spilling seasoned garlic nuts all over the cabin of the car, crumbs and spills are inevitable.

Small vehicle vacuums don't take up much space and are so easy to use. Get a vacuum that plugs into the twelve-volt outlet (the cigarette lighter) and use it whenever you're inspired. I like to start each day with a very quick once-over, just removing the prior day's crumbs and accumulated dirt.

While somebody else is prepping the picnic lunch or finishing breakfast with the kids, you or another in your travel group can be quickly cleaning up the cabin of your vehicle so everyone starts the journey on the right foot (and without crumbs).

One other important task to do each day (and I like to do it at the end of a day's drive) is empty any trash from inside the car. Banana peels and apple cores will bring fruit flies and bad smells. If you ate any takeout or drive-thru meals, be sure to have that all cleaned up and out as well. The smell of stale french fries is nobody's favorite, so definitely use the air freshening spray before you wrap up the car for the night.

VEHICLE ORIENTATION

As I said, I love doing a quick orientation with my travel group before beginning a road trip. During the first three or four minutes, we go through each area of the car reviewing what supplies and tools can be found where.

In addition to making sure everyone knows where plugs and charging cables are, we cover what snacks are where. This is a good time, especially if you're traveling with kids, to explain what food is earmarked or planned for which days. Example: You have a lovely box of artisan crackers in your dry snack bag. Those aren't for snack number one ten minutes from home but are part of the beautiful picnic spread you've put together for the next afternoon.

Vehicle orientation is also a good time to confirm that there is a waste receptacle, aka trash bag, accessible to each passenger. As you're showing everyone how you've got things organized, you can confirm everyone's understanding that trash *doesn't* belong on the floor. At any time. Ever.

I like to review what's in the cooler or trunk area of the car with everyone as well. Because we tend to have a few coolers, it's nice to have somebody else understand where things are kept. There's nothing like hangry passengers and the person driving being the only one who knows how to help them.

KEEPING FOOD FROM WILDLIFE

This book is not a guide to backwoods camping, but even on a road trip, you'll need to be aware of wildlife and how your food is stored. No, you don't have to hang your food from a tree at every rest stop, but you do need to be conscious of smart, hungry animals that may have been exposed to human food in the past.

As I tell my kids often, keep wildlife wild. Your picnic or snack isn't meant for wild animals. In addition to there being ingredients that can make wildlife sick, teaching animals that humans are a source of food hurts everyone:

- animals grow dependent on human food
- animals' nutritional needs aren't met
- humans can be harmed as animals become braver near them
- if a dangerous situation arises, wildlife may have to be relocated or, in some cases, put down

Don't share your food, and you can consider yourself to be actively doing your part.

When it comes to making sure animals can't get to the food in your car, typically proper food storage is fine. There are places where animal behavior or the lack of human exposure makes for its own interesting situation, and you'll know when you're someplace like that. For example: Many national and state parks will post warning signs about animal activity and some even provide food lockers to ensure animals don't damage cars trying to get to human food.

While places with food lockers tend to be primarily overnight camping areas, trailheads may also want you to take this precaution. Better safe than sorry, and that includes keeping wildlife safe.

CHAPTER 4

SAFETY

BASICS OF ROAD TRIP VEHICLE SAFETY

So you've decided to head out on a road trip! Road trips are such a great way to explore so many amazing places before getting to your destination. But with excitement comes a slew of potential problems that you need to be ready for.

Now, I don't want to scare you, but so many things can happen on the road. After countless road trips, both starting at home or with a rental car, we're always sure that vehicle safety is addressed before we leave.

PRE-TRIP CHECKLIST

Confirm you have the below critical items packed and that you complete these important checks before starting your car and leaving your drive-way. Ten minutes of thoughtful action may save you hours of despair later.

Current Registration and Proof of Insurance

It seems like a no-brainer to have your vehicle documentation in your car, but maybe you just renewed your tabs or just got your new proof of insurance and forgot to put them in the glove box. Better to check and make sure before ending up in a sticky situation. Also, clean out your glove box to make everything easily accessible in case you need to quickly find your documents.

This is also a great time to confirm if roadside assistance is included in your auto insurance, cell phone plan, or with one of your credit cards. Or join AAA or CAA.

Offline Maps and Apps

Thank goodness for technology, but boy is it a pain when it fails us. Before you head out on a road trip, be sure that you've downloaded offline maps for the area you're exploring. While it's rare to not be able to get a GPS signal, being far enough out that you can't get a digital map of your location can be a problem.

Take a few minutes while you have Wi-Fi or cell coverage to dig into your map program on your cell phone and download the offline map for the area. If you choose too large of an area, it'll use a ton of space on your phone, so just looking at your road trip route to see where you'll most likely be without coverage is a good approach to selecting your offline map.

Tip: If you know you're going to be out of cell coverage range, when you're plugging in your destination into your map app, set it up with your next destination in civilization as the final one, and with your next stop (remote hiking trail, perhaps) as a stop along the way. This way you'll get the full route downloaded even if you stop midway.

The same goes for other mapping or trail apps. Input your destination information or trail route in advance. You never want to be so lost that you start to worry or fear not finding your way back.

Spare Tire with Tools

All spare tires are different. Make sure you've got one on hand and make sure it's not flat! It's also a good idea to confirm you have the car jack and levers necessary to be able to use it in case of a damaged tire on the road.

This is a moment to be humble: If you don't know how to change a tire, either watch a YouTube video beforehand or ask somebody to show you how to do it. You can even stop by a car dealership or service station and they'll teach you. Stop into a police station for a spare tire inspection (like a car seat inspection).

There's no shame in making sure you can confidently change a tire.

Note: Even if you have roadside assistance service, you need to know how to fix a flat tire. If you're in a location with poor cell phone service and very few cars driving by, you need to be able to take care of yourself well enough to make it to a town with services.

Roadside Emergency Kit

You never want to be in an emergency, but if you are, it's good to be prepared. I strongly recommend putting together a roadside emergency kit (or buying one) that includes both vehicle and people supplies. Yes, I mentioned this in chapter 2, but it's important to repeat here, since you don't want to be caught without it.

It's critical that you get an emergency kit with jumper cables. I feel like I've used jumper cables more than any other item in my emergency kit. Plus, it feels good to be the hero for another stranded road tripper who didn't put together a road trip essentials kit and help them get back on the road!

Your roadside emergency kit should include:

- battery jumper cables
- at least three flares
- reflective triangles or small cones
- first-aid kit
- flashlight
- backup charger pack (for cell phone)
- nonperishable snacks
- drinking water
- water for vehicle engine

Simple Tool Kit

My father-in-law always impresses me. He's prepared for everything. He has a simple tool kit in his car at all times just in case he needs it for himself or someone else. It's got your screwdrivers, battery post cleaner, zip ties, and standard or metric socket set and wrench.

These are great to have on hand, just in case, even if you think you'll never need them.

Example: We were on a road trip and the skid plate (under the engine) came loose and was grinding on the ground. We were able to pull out our zip ties to secure it until we could get it fixed! Even if our safety wasn't compromised by this, the sound it made was annoying, and had it come off on the highway it might have struck the vehicle behind us, endangering them.

Another bonus to having a basic tool kit in your vehicle is having the ability to repair broken toys. Whether your child brought a radio-controlled car whose batteries are dead or you have to disassemble the reel on your fishing rod, basic tools come in handy more often than you could ever imagine.

Scheduled Maintenance

I like our car to be in its best condition it can be before embarking on a long road trip. I recommend taking your car in for service at your local garage or performing it yourself.

I always make sure all the lights work, the brakes are solid, the wipers are effective, and the fluids are fresh and topped off. Also, being sure the tires are prepped and ready to go versus ready to blow on the first strip of rough pavement is key to having a safe road trip.

Note: If your vehicle has any recalls due, get them taken care of before you head out on your road trip. While a lot of recalls are for small things that don't impact your safety, sometimes a recall is very important and ignoring it may be dangerous.

Snow Chains

Previously, I'd mentioned the need for snow chains in a well-built emergency kit. They really are important. If you're going to travel where there *might* be snow, make sure you've got your chains! So, what if you think July isn't the season for snow in the mountains? Leave them at home, and Mother Nature is like, "Hold my beer. They aren't prepared."

True, out-of-season snow isn't likely in most road trip destinations, but if you're visiting the Sierras or Rockies, storm systems can brew out of nothing and surprise you. And don't even get me started on Colorado, where we've woken up to snow the morning after an 85-degree day.

If you're doing a winter or spring road trip, having snow chains is extra

important. We were on a road trip to Sequoia National Park at the end of April. We knew there could be snow there since it's the mountains, so we had our chains. We didn't think we would actually need them because it was 75 degrees in the valley before we headed up into the park, but as we traveled up to Sequoia, the weather drastically changed, and it started dumping snow. Thankfully, we had our chains!

Tip: I recommend practicing putting on chains before you must use them. We've had a bit of a struggle getting our chains on in the snow every time we've needed to do it, but ultimately have always been successful because we've practiced.

QUICK HITS FOR SMALL BUT SERIOUS EMERGENCIES

What constitutes a small emergency when you're on a road trip? The *Oxford Advanced Learner's Dictionary* defines an *emergency* as "a sudden serious and dangerous event or situation which needs immediate action to deal with it."[1] I think we can agree that nobody wants to experience an emergency on the road, but just in case . . .

In the moment, some emergencies feel huge. An emergency might make you think that everything is going to spiral out of control and everything will have to end.

Remain Calm—Evaluate the Situation

First off, remain calm. Don't "calm down" but just remain calm. As you start to panic, your abilities to make both solid decisions and accurately assess your situation plummet.

If you find yourself stranded on the side of the highway, lost, remember: "This is momentary."

- Look for a road marker, such as a highway number *and* mile marker. If you don't have cell service, this will help you locate yourself on a physical map.
- Should you not have a paper map, drive on and keep an eye on your cell phone coverage until you have a small signal.
- Hang tight and sit outside your vehicle to signal a passing car as a last resort.

If you realize you left your wallet two hundred miles back at a gas station, remember: "I can drive back, and if I run out of gas, I can call for help."

- While losing your wallet or documents during travel is stressful, there are ways to work around a complete loss, including digital or paper copies in case of emergency.
- Keep a fair amount of cash in your vehicle in the event you lose access to your credit or debit cards. This way you can get gas, food, or even a hotel if things unravel.

If you've gotten a second flat tire and don't have another spare, remember: "I can call for help" or "Highway Patrol can help me."

- While this is a rare situation, it poses more danger than others. Taking action to ask for help quickly is important. If you don't have another spare tire, you *cannot* risk damaging your vehicle by continuing on.
- You can't put a price on safety, so if you need to call an expensive service station a hundred miles away, that's better than trying to make it just a bit farther and then having an accident.

There's always a calm solution that may indeed take a little time, but there's always a solution to get you out of a small but serious emergency.

Ways to Signal for Help

While most road trips won't take you out into the wild of the off-road tundra or unexplored desert, you may find yourself on a random dirt road far from civilization and in need of help. Should you be in an emergency situation, there are a few ways to signal for help, assuming you can't call somebody.

Remember that in any situation safety is the goal. If signaling for help brings undue danger on you or others, find a different method.

- Flag down traffic: This is the obvious choice, but also something to approach with caution. Yes, there are mysterious strangers on the road that you need to be wary of, but just being outside your car on a highway can also be dangerous. If you need to flag down traffic, stay close to your vehicle and allow yourself an escape route should another vehicle seem like it might hit you. Use a shirt or towel to make yourself bigger by waving it around (this will hopefully get attention sooner).

- Use flares: Properly using flares is key. When you open an emergency flare, it's easy to burn yourself, and you don't want to add a medical emergency to your current situation, so be careful. When you light a flare, place it safely away from your vehicle between you and oncoming traffic. The combination of smoke and light from the flare is ideal for getting attention near and far.

- Leverage vehicle lights: As soon as you know there's a problem, put on your hazard lights. This lets people see you and keeps you safe, as well as signals that there is a problem. If you need to, you can also use your headlights to signal for help if you're at a high point in the road.

- Build a signal fire: This is your last resort and is for an emergency situation where there is little to no chance of anyone driving by or finding you unintentionally. Find a place as close to your vehicle as is safe to start a small signal fire (using a lighter or matches from your emergency roadside kit). Be sure that you can contain the flames and ash so that a larger fire doesn't start, and be sure to have a pile of dirt and rocks at the ready to put the fire out when needed. **This is your last resort**.

Hopefully you won't need to take any of these actions. If you do, though, be wise, be calm, and be patient. In the next section, we'll cover tools and services to help you during road trip emergencies.

Travel Tools and Services for Road Trip Emergencies

Peace of mind is my favorite item to pack for a road trip, and that looks different for everyone. Having the right tools and services in case of emergency is where I start.

The basics before heading out on a road trip include:

- emergency plan
- emergency roadside kit
- handheld battery-operated radio (in case of a weather disaster)
- paper maps, bought or printed
- battery powerpack/charger pack

Building an Emergency Plan

When I'm getting a vehicle ready for a road trip, whether we're bringing our camping trailer or just driving our car, I'm always sure to have an emergency plan for any sort of mishap. The emergency plan includes important phone numbers we may need (roadside assistance, bank, telehealth doctor, hotels along the route, etc.), and also has a copy of our itinerary with any coordinating phone number, which may include people we know near our locations.

The reason for collecting a few hotel phone numbers along the route is so that should you be in an emergency situation, you can call a hotel both for support and to secure a room if you're not near your planned stopping point. Having worked in hotels for many years, I can confirm that *every* hotel has local recommendations or people who can help a potential guest in an emergency.

Telehealth has become a wonderful tool for getting medical advice without being close to your doctor. Most medical insurance providers have a variety of options for this, including video calling with a doctor. Find this information before you leave on your trip, and if there is an app or service you need to sign up for in advance, complete that before you actually need it.

Have you ever been traveling and then your credit card stops working? Or maybe you're trying to pay a tow truck driver and your card gets declined? Yeah, those are emergency situations of their own, but they can really put a halt to your road trip. Before you leave, be sure to let your bank know that you'll be traveling and get their twenty-four-hour support number.

Tales from the Road: We were driving across the US towing our camping trailer, so getting really poor gas mileage. On day two of filling up the tank every 140 miles or so, our credit card got declined. We thought it was an error, so we used another one . . . which then started getting declined too! After calling both banks, we found that so many purchases at gas stations in such a short amount of time is a signal of irregular and suspicious behavior. Thank goodness for that third credit card we could use for the next day while our banks removed the holds.

Yes, there are phone numbers on credit cards for basic inquiries, but many banks have additional customer service lines to support emergency situations, such as theft or accessing money out of the ordinary. Get those numbers into your plan!

My emergency plan is sometimes printed out and sometimes it's a collection of notes on my smartphone. When I make an emergency plan, I'm sure to make it easily and quickly accessible. For that reason, having a paper backup is always a good idea.

Rental Car Emergency Roadside Kit

An emergency roadside kit is *so very important*. Do not leave on a road trip without one, including if you're not using your own car. If you're renting a car, you still need to be sure to have emergency supplies. See the Versatile Road Trip Gear section for a detailed packing list.

As a standard, rental vehicles will come with a basic kit: spare tire and jack, flares and reflectors, and the vehicle manual (in glove compartment). Some rental agencies might also provide jumper cables or allow you to rent a complete kit.

You can easily prepare yourself a bit better by stopping at a store before you've left civilization to collect the following, which you most likely didn't pack in your airline luggage:

- first-aid kit
- flashlight
- backup charger pack (for cell phone)
- nonperishable snacks
- drinking water
- water for vehicle engine

Additionally, if you're renting a car, double-check with your credit card company what sort of coverage they provide as far as additional insurance or support if you use that card for the rental.

Using Paper Maps

There are parts of me that will never go fully digital. Yes, I absolutely use the map app on my smartphone and its vehicle integration features when I'm on a road trip, but technology is fallible. Paper maps are a safety net I will never be without.

I remember learning how to read and actually use paper maps in school as a child. The skills of finding mile markers, understanding types of roads, and calculating distance still suit me today. True, I often use them more with hiking maps, but still I use them.

When you're collecting paper maps for a road trip, try to get them narrowed down to the region you're spending the most remote time in.

For example: If you're exploring Grand Staircase-Escalante National Monument in Utah, you'll see that there are many dead zones between Bryce Canyon and Capitol Reef National Parks. A paper map is extremely helpful if you want to explore anything off your direct route.

Printing paper maps with step-by-step instructions is also a good way to prepare for areas without coverage. Using your preferred online mapping tool, you can print out your complete route, and you can even zoom into areas you may want to explore that aren't detailed in your itinerary.

Helpful Emergency Services

Again, the hope is that you never need any of these, but in the event that you do . . .

Products that are built into vehicles, such as OnStar or SiriusXM, are easy ways to be sure you have access to emergency services. These technologies provide a connection to both call centers (emergency services) and sudden weather events (in-vehicle alerts). But not all cars have these. That's where digging into services you already use is helpful.

You can, of course, just sign up for roadside assistance or a service like AAA/CAA, but you may not have to. I've used roadside assistance through my cell service provider, my credit card company, my travel insurance, and my regular auto insurance. While not every one of these services offers this specific perk or coverage, many do or allow you to elect for it to be a part of your membership/agreement.

Another emergency service you may need is in-person medical assistance. Either before your trip or when the situation arises, contact your medical provider for in-network or preferred providers in the area you're visiting. Emergency medical expenses can be astronomical in the US, so being prepared with a plan that's within your insurance network is a smart action that may save you mountains of stress or costs down the road.

DIY VEHICLE FIXES IN AN EMERGENCY

There are things you can do on the road to make sure you can get to safety if something goes wrong with your vehicle. Beyond knowing how to fix a flat tire, you can actually do several small things yourself to patch up a problem on the road.

In any situation that isn't completely obvious and easy, always refer to the vehicle manual (in the glove compartment) for troubleshooting or instructions. Also, it's okay to call for help if you truly don't know where to begin or think it's more serious than not.

The following are the most basic things you can do if you think your car is "having a moment," or if you know there's something wrong.

Flat Tire: Change It

Changing a flat tire can be stressful, even if you've done it before. It may be that you've popped a tire or possibly just have been leaking air and it's nearly flat. Either situation is unsafe. Here is the simplest process to fix it:

1. Pull over to a safe, flat area with hard ground
2. Set up reflectors or flares to alert other drivers to your presence outside your car
3. Place jack under vehicle, feeling first for the *solid frame*, not the door or the bumper
4. Jack up the vehicle high enough to see that the tire is off the ground
5. Remove lug nuts with tire iron (may be a part of the jack system)
6. Remove tire and replace with spare
7. Tighten all lug nuts
8. Place flat tire in spare compartment
9. Drive with caution to get a new tire

That may seem like a lot of steps, but in all things, safety first.

Overheating: Cool It

With newer vehicles, overheating happens very infrequently, but if your car has a vintage vibe or even a 1990s throwback feel to it, you may experience overheating during a long drive.

Ideally, having engine coolant on hand will make the process of adding coolant easy, but if you don't have any in your vehicle, adding a bit of water to the coolant reservoir is okay. You don't want to load it up with water, as a hot engine may make water boil, but you can add water to coolant to keep it effective until you can add the proper fluid.

This is only a temporary fix and *is not* how you maintain a vehicle. This is *only* suggested if you're in a pinch and your car is overheating.

Poor Visibility: Replace It

Driving with poor visibility can be difficult and dangerous. On a long road trip you'd be surprised how many things can impact your visibility:

- bugs
- mud
- dust
- snow
- rain
- cracks in the windshield

While replacing a whole windshield may not be a good solution during your road trip, you can stop in and get cracks sealed if it's appropriate. That's not the solution for all cracks but is sometimes what you must do based on timing and budget.

The other issues can easily be addressed either with windshield wipers or headlights. Both of these are easy fixes that somebody at an auto parts store can even help you with if needed. Bad windshield wipers or a dead headlight can severely impact driving safety or could even get you pulled over by highway patrol.

Spend a few dollars, pull into a small town for a quick minute, and fix your visibility problems.

Squealing or Smoking: Service It

And here's where we draw the line with DIY vehicle fixes. Unless you're an auto mechanic, I don't recommend messing around with belts, caps, and other moving pieces while you're on a road trip. The goal here is making your vehicle safer, not testing your rusty or nonexistent auto shop skills in the middle of nowhere.

Oftentimes, getting your vehicle serviced, even with just an oil change, can solve potential problems with squealing or smoking. If a belt is going bad, a quick service will find it and a mechanic can replace it for you. If the car is smoking, perhaps there is a leak or spill that's causing it, or maybe there is a part to replace. Again, getting an oil change or simple service may provide you a solution swiftly to get back on the road safely.

In any case, nobody needs to try to be a hero when it comes to road trip safety. Fix the things you know you can and use the tools and services at your disposal for the things you can't.

RESEARCHING ROAD CONDITIONS

I think we can agree that a large number of road trips happen in the summer. You know what else happens a lot in the summer? Road construction. And a lot of people travel for the holidays too, such as Thanksgiving or Christmas. And that's usually when snow starts to fall.

Before your departure day, and during your road trip as well, it's important to do a bit of research regarding road conditions and potential problems along your route. Of course, you'll be traveling with an emergency roadside kit, but you'll still want to practice safety before it's even required.

ROAD CONDITIONS TO WATCH FOR

Just like there are a variety of road types or different environments you might drive through, there are a lot of different road conditions and hazards to be aware of. There might also sometimes be laws that vary based on the road condition.

Construction Zones

I wish there was a way to always avoid construction zones, but it's just not 100 percent possible. Road construction zones can cause massive delays even when you know that they're coming up. If you're driving along and you start to see construction signs, or you're using a driving app that alerts you, sometimes it's good to take your own detour to avoid unnecessary delays.

If we are on a road trip and see an active construction zone coming up *and* it's rush hour, we'll proactively get off the highway and either find a park or eat dinner early so that we aren't sitting in traffic longer than we need to.

Yes, there are times when you just have to wait for construction crews to guide you through, and most commonly this will be on rural roads that have been switched to one lane. In this situation, you just have to be patient and know that when things get moving, you get to continue your amazing road trip.

Note: If you're stopping for a long period of time, don't idle your engine. Not only is this bad for the planet but you'll also waste gas and run the risk of overheating your car. If you're sitting for a long time and it's cold, use your best judgment about starting your car to warm your crew.

Another thing to be aware of if you have an exceptionally long delay due to construction is your lights being left on and killing your battery. Today's cars have much better energy efficiency than older vehicles (throwback to station wagon road trips of the 1980s!), but you still don't want to put undue stress on your car.

→ Proactively Research Construction Zones

Before your road trip, do a bit of research. Luckily for travelers, destinations and governments often publish construction updates and warnings on their websites now. If you're visiting a national park, jump on the internet before you leave and you'll usually see road closures and predictions for travel obstacles on the national park site and can plan your travel around that.

Another way to scope out potential construction delays is to map your route in a driving app before you leave on your road trip. Zoom in along your path and look at sections of the route that have either construction symbols or red and orange lines indicating bad traffic. If you know what lies ahead, you can adjust what time you'll be driving through or find an alternative route.

Another thing to look for on government sites is any notice about weather preparation. In northern climates, this will often take place at the end of summer with patch work happening in spring. If you're traveling in a state or province with its own Department of Transportation app, download it and keep an eye on the alerts.

Tales from the Road: Double Flats on the ALCAN

Once upon a time I was driving the ALCAN, aka the Alaska Highway, and I knew that a fair portion was dirt road. In fact, I'd already driven the length of the ALCAN heading south at the end of that summer, just before

the first snow came. The crews had already started prepping the highway for winter, which included regrading the roads. Around three o'clock in the afternoon, I got a flat tire and had to put on the spare, still about eighty miles from the next town. Not more than half an hour later, I had another tire start to go flat and still wasn't close to town. I drove slowly and carefully as the second tire leaked, just making it to the service station. Thankfully they were able to repair both tires, which had picked up sharp pieces of metal from the grader blade that had been working on the road before us.

Weather Impacting Road Conditions

Driving in the rain isn't always a bad thing. Some vehicles handle it very well and some don't. There are ways to make sure you're safe on the road even if you can't necessarily prevent driving in the rain. And it's the same for driving in snowy conditions; they may happen, but you can make sure you're ready.

Before any road trip, you should always make sure your vehicle is running in tiptop shape, which often means a tune-up or servicing. If you're not getting professional service on your car, you can double-check a few things yourself:

- Make sure your headlights, high beams, and fog lights (if you have them) are all working and angled properly at the road.
- Confirm that your washer fluid is full and that your windshield wipers are in good condition.
- Examine your tires for ABCs: abrasions, bumps, or cuts. If there is a problem with a tire, get it fixed before you're on the road.
- Review your snow chain situation and confirm that you know and understand how to put them on if needed.

Really, the best way to combat weather and its effect on road conditions is to be prepared and stay alert. Also, if you feel unsafe driving or feel that conditions are worsening, get off the road to a safe place. Driving and endangering yourself or others is no form of being a road trip hero.

Unplanned Unpaved Roads

Good old-fashioned paper maps, in comparison to modern digital maps, often have better legends that define road types and the visuals of different textured lines. Why is this important? Well, have you followed a digital map in your car lately and ended up on a pothole-filled gravel road in the middle of nowhere? I have.

Unfortunately, weather can really take a toll on pavement, sometimes even causing it to deteriorate or wash away in full or in part. When it comes to road repairs, there is usually a lengthy process and part of that is removing a layer of pavement, which can take quite a while and leave the road as bare gravel. And that gravel can stretch for miles and may even be in that condition for more than a year.

The other gravel or unpaved road to be wary of is the road built for recreational vehicles versus automobiles. Yes, I've followed my digital map instructions and it's taken me onto snowmobile routes . . . from which I had to be rescued by a tow truck . . . deep in the woods.

When you come across unplanned unpaved roads, it's a very good idea to look at your map and find an alternate route. Sometimes there won't be one and you just have to proceed with caution, but if you can avoid the danger and uncertainty of a rough road, do it.

Tales from the Road: Snowmobile Route Surprise

My family and I were on a road trip through Nova Scotia (great travel plan in the Itineraries chapter!) when we landed ourselves in a more rural area than we'd been driving through. Our online map sent us down a farm road that soon turned into a bumpier path than we'd expected. Since this was a tight roadway, we couldn't turn around easily. I decided to slowly continue, thinking perhaps it was just a rough patch, but the road quickly went downhill—very steeply downhill. Despite our having stopped almost immediately, the rough road and wet fall leaves made backing up impossible.

We walked down the road, and then I left my family and walked much farther back toward the start until I got cell phone service. Eventually a tow truck with a winch showed up and pulled us back up the apparent snowmobile trail. Yes, there was a small sign about a quarter mile before our stranding point that said it was for snowmobiles, but our map didn't know that. Argh!

RESOURCES FOR CURRENT ROAD CONDITIONS

As I mentioned, local government and tourism websites have become excellent resources for up-to-date information on road conditions. Additionally, Department of Transportation (DOT) apps are becoming more and more common. Use these free tools to stay current with the road ahead.

The following are the most reliable resources to make sure your road trip travel is safe and that you're leveraging the best roads to get from point A to point B:

- state/provincial DOT websites
- national and state park website alerts
- DOT apps
- GPS apps: these often have real-time road conditions and alerts
- local tourism websites

One more way to find out about the road ahead is to ask hotel staff or local law enforcement if there's anything to be aware of before you head out. Local word of mouth has saved us on many occasions in foreign territory.

Use your resources and make wise decisions. The goal of a road trip is to have great experiences, so do the work to make sure they're all great instead of having horror stories to share when you get home.

NIGHT DRIVING

I usually avoid driving at night in general, and going on road trips is no different. Night driving presents its own set of precautions and dangers, and honestly, I don't want to worry about those things, but sometimes on a road trip you have to.

I plan my family's travel to include as little night driving as possible. When it does occur, though, here's how we make sure to stay safe.

SAFE NIGHT DRIVING PRACTICES AND PRECAUTIONS

While you may be at the mercy of a car rental facility if you're flying to the start of your road trip destination, you can still take steps to be sure you're as safe as possible on the road. Whether you leave from your driveway or the airport, follow these tips to keep you and your traveling companions safe while driving at night.

Headlight Maintenance

Just as with bad weather and sketchy road conditions, one of the easiest ways to be sure you're safe driving at night is by making sure your headlights are working properly. This doesn't just mean that your running lights are functioning, but that your headlights are at full power and actually pointed at the road.

That's right, read it again: *pointed at the road*. If you've never driven a car with one headlight (or both) improperly angled, consider yourself lucky. Not only are wonky headlights irritating, they're really unsafe.

Before having your first night driving experience on unfamiliar roads, try to confirm your lights are both working and properly angled.

- Pull forward to a parking spot in front of a wall and see if the beams are level when you're really close. As you back up, watch to be sure they remain level. The true test is once you're on the road, but this trick can help prevent issues later.

In addition to your headlights, make sure your taillights are working too. You'll want to have a partner to test them with you or back up close to a wall and use the mirror.

- While you're parked with your foot off the brake, confirm that your taillights are working. While watching the lights (or having a friend watch), tap the brakes and make sure the lights clearly get brighter.

While you're responsible for your own night driving, you want to be sure you're being safe for other drivers too.

Proper Use of High Beams for Night Driving

I admit, I'm terrible at remembering when I have my high beams on. When I'm on a rural road and it's dark, it usually takes a passing car or two to remind me that I have my brights on. So, how do you make sure you're being courteous to other drivers and not blinding them as they drive by?

I always ask my passenger to remind me that my brights are on. I know that may seem silly, but it's worth it. A lot of drivers flash their brights at oncoming cars that still have their high beams on, and at night, that extra blinding light is just not safe. Thus, I prefer to have somebody help me remember to turn off my brights instead of the constant flashes.

Watching for Wildlife at Night

Hitting a deer or a moose will most likely total your car. While we can't predict when wildlife will jump out into the road at night, you can proactively watch for wildlife. Something amazing about creatures who are active after dark is their reflective eyes. There have been very few times that I've had wildlife jump out in front of my car at night where I didn't get a split second of a clue they were there first.

Again, ask your copilot to keep their eyes out for wildlife as you're driving at night. This may mean asking them to not be on their phone or maybe it's asking them to stay awake, but either way, the extra set of eyes is worth it.

Note: Asking for an extra set of eyes is also great during daytime driving. I'm thrown back to a crazy moment on a rural Florida road when a wild boar jumped in front of my car and my passenger's exclamation saved us from both hitting the boar and/or wrecking the car.

Healthy Eyes and Eyewear

I don't think that it's just my eyes that get blurry as they get tired. Keeping your eyes healthy and strong on a road trip is very important. If you're tired enough that your eyes aren't clear or you start to doze, or even think about dozing, you need to *stop* driving. This is a great opportunity to either ask somebody else to drive or to pull over where it's safe.

The other side of that is making sure that if you wear glasses, either every day or in certain scenarios, that they are readily available. I have an astigmatism in one eye, and when I'm really focused or driving at night, the effect of the astigmatism is much worse and my right eye just doesn't want to cooperate. That's when wearing my glasses really helps, because my eyes can stop straining and I can focus much better.

If you don't have another person to ask to drive and you feel you need to keep going, pulling over somewhere safe and well-lit can sometimes be of great help. The burst of energy from changing your body position or breathing fresh, cool air can really help as well.

Ultimately, if your eyes are strained and you're getting tired, you should not be driving at night. Be safe, be smart.

Clean Windshield, Clear View

Have you ever noticed how oncoming lights refract across every bug smear and drop of mud on your windshield? It's true. Dirt and grime on your windshield can present quite the visual obstacle when driving at night. Besides not having a clear view in general, the light from oncoming cars is much more widespread and intense when it's coming through a dirty windshield.

The easiest fix for a dirty windshield is to keep it clean, but that takes more than just washer fluid. Good windshield wiper blades paired with washer fluid can make a big difference if you have to clean your windshield at night.

Note: If you have a really bad bug problem in front of your face, you may need to actually pull into a gas station to clean your windshield by hand. Yes, it's going to take you off course for a few minutes, but that's okay in the name of safety.

PROPER PLANNING AND TIME MANAGEMENT

I know that the daily plan or schedule can get a bit off kilter. I'm guilty of spending two hours longer on a hike than I planned. I'm guilty of getting distracted by a dirt road that was calling my name, but I always try to plan for those uncertainties.

Budgeting Time to Prevent Night Driving

When you're first building your road trip itinerary and looking at how long you want to spend driving and doing daily activities, this is where you can build in a safety net to prevent night driving. When you're actually making a plan, be honest with yourself about how long different activities will take and then overestimate it when you're actually scheduling the day.

Example: You arrive at a trailhead for a hike that you think will take two hours. Plan that it will actually take three hours so that you have a little buffer built in as your day continues.

If you're scheduling down to the minute, just stop. Make your schedule to be more flexible with each activity. What's the worst that can happen? You arrive at your hotel an hour early and actually get to relax or explore the destination on foot a bit?

Planning for Daylight Hours

Ha! There's a bonus to flying to a road trip destination! If you're flying from Florida to do a road trip around Maine, did you know that in the summer the sun is up nearly three hours later than it sets in Florida? And it rises earlier too!

And the reverse is also true. If you're traveling from the North and doing a road trip along a southern route, expect the sun to go down quite a bit earlier than you're used to. In spring and fall, it's much more even across the latitudes, but in summer and winter, you get the extreme span of daylight hours.

Take this into account as you plan your daily drive times and activities.

Adjusting Schedules to Avoid Driving at Night

It's okay to have gone off the plan a bit; don't worry. If you find that you're driving at night when you don't feel comfortable or safe doing so, there are ways to fix that. Here are five ways to adjust your schedule to prevent night driving:

→ Change your starting time each day

If you get up an hour earlier, will you reach your final stop for the day before night driving begins? I love to wake up early in general and when I'm on a road trip, I find that getting up early gets me energized for the day, and on trips through wild areas, I see a lot more wildlife.

Spend less time dining. That might sound strange, but sit-down dining experiences, while wonderful, can really add up when it comes to time. You're better off picnicking or grabbing food to go than having a complete sit-down restaurant experience for breakfast or lunch. Shaving off forty-five minutes to an hour by not having a dine-in meal will both keep you on track and save you money.

→ Cut an activity from your schedule

I really don't like this option, but sometimes making a responsible choice for our health and safety means missing out on something. If you think you need to do this, figure it out ASAP. Ideally, you can plan to cut something out the day before it was planned, but sometimes you need to change your plans on the fly. Be flexible. Be forgiving. Enjoy what you *do* get to do.

→ Adjust where you spend the night

This can be trickier than other options as sometimes you either have prepaid for a hotel stay or there actually isn't another lodging option closer than what you've got planned. Before you decide to change your endpoint for the day, make sure you can secure other accommodations. It would be frustrating to change your evening plan only to discover that you had to stick with the original final destination.

→ Rethink the whole plan

Let's say you're a day or two into your road trip and you can tell you haven't allocated enough time to both do what you want to do and drive from place to place. This is when you really do need to reconsider your complete plan. If there are a few key sights or places you've been looking forward to, shift things to make sure you can still do those activities.

Tales from the Road: Delayed Departure, Long Nights

As a travel writer, I like to think that people get to learn from my mistakes so that they have better life experiences. Listen here: On your primary travel day to your starting destination, *have zero plans*. That's right. Plan to get to your starting hub and nothing else. If you have extra time, that's just a bonus.

Why is that? Well, have you ever been stuck in Phoenix with continually delayed flights for eight hours straight? If you have, you get it. When you're flying to the start of a road trip, you need to plan to do nothing but get your rental car and have a good night's sleep, and then you can start your road trip fresh the next morning. If you're not flying but just delayed in leaving home, keeping that first afternoon or evening of travel free allows for errors or mistakes in timing judgment.

In the situation above, I was stuck in Phoenix with my son, trying to get to Seattle to start a road trip around the Olympic Peninsula, and our flights just kept getting delayed. We ended up landing in Seattle after dark and driving more than three hours, dead tired. Had we planned properly, we would've been fine landing in Seattle, sleeping, and then starting early the next day. Lesson learned. We did safely make it to our family and our trip proceeded the next morning.

In the end, what's important is that you can be flexible and travel in a way that is both enjoyable and safe.

SAFETY RESOURCES

The following safety resources may prove helpful if you're traveling and find yourself in trouble. While modern roadside assistance technology is incredible, it's not a standard feature on every vehicle.

Before beginning your trip, be sure that you have the contact information for highway safety or your local roadside assistance provider. Remember, if you're driving across a border—say, into Canada or Mexico—your normal roadside coverage may not be available should you have an emergency. If nothing else, be sure that your cell phone will function properly for emergency calls, and that you know who to call for support in another country.

→ **US Transportation Emergency Services by State**

	DEPT. OF TRANSPORTATION	STATE NONEMERGENCY
ALABAMA (AL)	334-353-6554	800-832-5660
ALASKA (AK)	907-465-8952	511
ARIZONA (AZ)	602-712-7355	511
ARKANSAS (AR)	501-569-2000	501-569-2374
CALIFORNIA (CA)	916-654-2852	800-835-5247
COLORADO (CO)	511	303-239-4500
CONNECTICUT (CT.)	N/A	911 (INCLUDES NONEMERGENCY DISPATCH)
DELAWARE (DE)	800-652-5600	302-739-4863
FLORIDA (FL)	511	347
GEORGIA (GA)	404-631-1990	511
HAWAII (HI)	808-831-6714	808-935-3311
IDAHO (ID)	208-334-8000	*477
ILLINOIS (IL)	800-452-4368	911 (INCLUDES NONEMERGENCY DISPATCH)
INDIANA (IN)	855-463-6848	317-232-8248
IOWA (IA)	800-288-1047	800-525-5555
KANSAS (KS)	511	785-296-6800
KENTUCKY (KY)	N/A	502-782-1800
LOUISIANA (LA)	511	225-925-6006
MAINE (ME)	N/A	800-452-4664
MARYLAND (MD)	410-582-5650	800-525-5555

MASSACHUSETTS (MA)	511	508-820-2300
MICHIGAN (MI)	888-296-4546	517-284-3745
MINNESOTA (MN)	800-542-0220	651-201-7100
MISSISSIPPI (MS)	511	228-539-4881
MISSOURI (MO)	888-275-6636	573-751-3313
MONTANA (MT)	511	406-444-3780
NEBRASKA (NE)	511	800-525-5555
NEVADA (NV)	877-687-6237	775-687-5300
NEW HAMPSHIRE (NH)	603-271-6862	603-271-1162
NEW JERSEY (NJ)	511	609-882-2000
NEW MEXICO (NM)	505-795-1401	505-841-9256
NEW YORK (NY)	518-457-6195	914-834-9111
NORTH CAROLINA (NC)	877-368-4968	919-733-7952
NORTH DAKOTA (ND)	701-328-2598	800-472-2121
OHIO (OH)	614-466-7170	#677
OKLAHOMA (OK)	405-522-8000	405-425-2424
OREGON (OR)	503-986-3435	800-452-7888
PENNSYLVANIA (PA)	717-412-5300	717-783-5599
RHODE ISLAND (RI)	401-222-2378	401-444-1000
SOUTH CAROLINA (SC)	855-467-2368	803-896-9621
SOUTH DAKOTA (SD)	511	605-773-3105
TENNESSEE (TN)	511	*847
TEXAS (TX)	800-452-9292	512-424-2000
UTAH (UT)	801-965-4000	801-965-4518
VERMONT (VT)	802-917-2458	802-244-8727

VIRGINIA (VA)	800-367-7623	804-674-2000
WASHINGTON (WA)	511 OR 800-695-7623	360-596-4000
WEST VIRGINIA (WV)	800-964-1449	304-746-2100
WISCONSIN (WI)	511	844-847-1234
WYOMING (WY)	307-777-4375	307-777-4321

→ **Canadian Transportation Emergency Services by Province**

ALBERTA (AB)	511	780-423-4567
BRITISH COLUMBIA (BC)	250-387-3198	604-717-3321
MANITOBA (MB)	866-626-4862	204-983-5420
NEW BRUNSWICK (NB)	511	888-506-7267
NEWFOUNDLAND AND LABRADOR (NL)	709-729-2300	800-709-7267
NORTHWEST TERRITORIES (NWT)	867-767-9087	867-765-3900
NOVA SCOTIA (NS)	511	800-803-7267
NUNAVUT (NVT)	888-975-5999	867-975-4409
ONTARIO (ON)	511	888-310-1122
PRINCE EDWARD ISLAND (PEI)	902-368-5120	902-566-7112
QUEBEC (QC)	511	800-771-5401
SASKATCHEWAN (SK)	844-754-4929	306-310-7267
YUKON (YT)	867-667-8250	867-667-5555

— CHAPTER 5 —

ITINERARIES

TEN US ROAD TRIPS YOU
DEFINITELY SHOULDN'T MISS

I'm sure there are ten million different road trips you could construct for exploring the USA. I've done many myself, but for sure cannot claim all of them. That said, with years and years on the road, I feel confident making recommendations of my absolute favorites.

The following may not be the top-ranked road trips in the US, but they are certainly incredible and should not be missed. Take a page out of my book (not literally) and choose a few to conquer this year. No doubt you'll love the adventure and head off into the sunset with unforgettable memories.

As you pick an itinerary, consider what time you've set aside or will be setting aside. Trips longer than five days can easily be split into two parts, and any road trip plan can be extended by adding an extra day of relaxing or exploring locally.

To make any of these trips more budget friendly, plan them as far in advance as you're able, prepaying for hotels along the way. This will keep you more on schedule than you might prefer but will add a layer of safety in that you'll have secured accommodations for each night.

Remember before you hit the road:

- Have a plan, lax or strict, just so you can keep moving
- Have a goal so you can feel accomplished

- Be prepared with emergency basics, even if it's just adding roadside assistance to your insurance or cell phone plan
- Communicate with your world, share some check-in points for safety
- Have fun finding new experiences!

When you begin your road trip, whichever itinerary you choose, be sure to confirm that parks and sights are open for visitation. Guided tours may not be available at all places on all days, and some sights you'll need to visit earlier or later in the day based on when they close. Take operating hours and the season into consideration as you head out exploring.

Also, many road trips in the United States include visits to national parks or national park sights. If you don't have one already, be sure to get a National Parks Passport and collect the stamps and cancelations as you explore. This is one of the best souvenirs you can get in the USA and you'll use it for the rest of your life.

BEST OF OREGON

We probably shouldn't start here because this is the road trip that puts all other road trips to shame, but here we go.

Oregon: So often misunderstood and misrepresented. Oregon is the patch of earth that melds twenty-first-century-organic, off-the-grid individuals with 1950s classic black-and-white photographers. Oregon is full of pristine beaches, but it's also the high desert with coyotes howling into the night.

Start: Fly into Portland, OR (PDX)

Day 1: Explore Portland's fun, eclectic restaurant scene. Walk through the Pearl District and enjoy a farmers' market or the funky, punk style of the Urban Air Market. **Sleep in:** Portland

Day 2: Head west out of the city toward Astoria. Here you'll find a collection of Victorian homes, some interesting historic sites (like the Flavel House), and the start of the *Goonies* trail. Set in Astoria and down the coast, the best movie of the 1980s was filmed here. Spend the night down in Seaside, where you can wake up at the beach and feel like you're in another world. **Sleep in:** Seaside

Day 3: Continue down the coast, visiting more *Goonies* sights, including Ecola State Park in Cannon Beach. As you head to your endpoint in Newport, make stops at Cape Meares Lighthouse, the Tillamook Cheese Factory, Pacific City for beers on the beach, and Lincoln City. Watch the clock because it's easy to get distracted and spend hours watching the waves crash. **Sleep in:** Newport

Day 4: Wake up and head for the Yaquina Head Lighthouse where you can enjoy Oregon's nautical history and watch for whales. As you continue down the coast, make stops at Sea Lion Caves, Cape Perpetua for a short hike, and Old Town Florence for a seafood lunch. Enjoy the epic sand dunes with a climb at Honeyman Memorial State Park. Going a little off track, make your way to Shore Acres State Park for both a stunning view of the Cape Arago Lighthouse and to watch thirty-foot waves crash into the rocks and sea caves below. Amazing sight. **Sleep in:** Gold Beach

Day 5: Time to head inland with a stop at Oregon Caves National Monument and Preserve. Yes, you will have to drive through a bit of California, so make a stop in Jedediah Smith Redwoods State Park to walk among the giant trees. Tour the Oregon Caves and Chateau at the National Monument and then head east to Grants Pass. This is the start of wine country, so feel free to make a stop and have a glass. **Sleep in:** Roseburg

Day 6: Get ready for contrast, because after breakfast in Roseburg (cute town!) you head across the Cascade Mountains on the Thundering Waters Trail. As you go, make stops at the many waterfalls, including Toketee and Watson Falls. You'll cover a lot of ground before arriving at Newberry National Volcanic Monument, where waterfalls and hiking through an obsidian flow (huge glass rocks) make for a once-in-a-lifetime experience. **Sleep in:** Bend

Day 7: Explore Bend for the first part of the day, enjoying the riverwalk or hiking along the Deschutes River at Dillon Falls. Have lunch at one of the many breweries before going north to Terrebonne, where a hike at Smith Rock State Park awaits you. When you're done, hop in the car to catch sunset at the Painted Hills Overlook. **Sleep in:** Mitchell

Day 8: Either start by heading back to the Painted Hills Unit of John Day Fossil Beds National Monument or head to the Blue Basin for hiking in an otherworldly landscape. From here, enjoy the sleepy towns of Fossil and the ghost town of Shaniko. Get to Hood River for dinner and poke around downtown or watch windsurfers on the river. **Sleep in:** Hood River

Day 9: From Hood River, enjoy many stops along Historic Route 30 as you explore the Columbia River Gorge National Scenic Area. Stop and enjoy a stroll to the footbridge at Multnomah Falls, then a short hike at Latourell Falls and Oneonta Gorge. Finish with the view from Vista House of the majestic Columbia River. **Sleep in:** Troutdale or Portland

Day 10: You have two options for your last day. Head west to Willamette Valley for wine country tours and tastings, ending the night in the Portland area; or you can head east to explore Silver Falls State Park (if you haven't gotten enough waterfalls on this trip). On your way back from Silver Falls, stop at Leach Botanical Garden for moss-covered beauty before you're back in the city. **Sleep in:** Portland area

Depart: Leave from Portland, OR (PDX)

MOUNTAINS TO SEA IN CALIFORNIA

You may have read about our epic towering trees road trip in the chapter about planning. Well, *this is that trip*! This is the California road trip that really brings you the best of nature and California culture.

Start: Fly into San Francisco Bay Area (SFO, OAK, SJC): Spend the night in the Bay Area

Day 1: Leave San Francisco early by crossing the Golden Gate Bridge to Marin County. Your first stop is at Muir Woods National Monument, aka the Forest Moon of Endor, for a hike among the redwoods. Continue north through wine country stopping in Healdsburg for wine tasting and a meal. Continue through wine country to Ukiah. Stay here to relax and explore or drive on to Eureka. **Sleep in:** Ukiah or Eureka (two hours farther)

Day 2: Spend the morning exploring a bit of Victorian Eureka, the gateway to the redwoods, and then head north to Lady Bird Johnson Grove in Redwoods National Park. Enjoy some beach time, drive through a redwood tree or two, and then head back to Eureka for the night. The food scene in Eureka is surprisingly vibrant, like in a large metropolitan city, so be sure to enjoy a nice meal. **Sleep in:** Eureka

Day 3: Driving to Lassen Volcanic National Park is a gorgeous adventure. Make stops along the way to enjoy the rivers and grab lunch and snacks for later when you drive through Redding. Arrive at Mount Lassen around lunchtime to check out the Sulphur Works, Boiling Springs Lake, and other hydrothermal areas. **Sleep in:** Mineral, Chester, or drive to Reno (+ two hours)

Day 4: Yes, we've left California (but just temporarily). From Reno you're heading to Lake Tahoe, where you can either take the eastern or western route. On the east, make a stop at Sand Harbor or Secret Cove, or on the west explore D. L. Bliss State Park. Both offer some of the clearest waters in Lake Tahoe and are dotted with the iconic boulders near the shore. Grab lunch in South Lake Tahoe before you continue on to Mono Lake. Enjoy the sights of the saltwater lake and its bizarre geologic wonders. **Sleep in:** Mono or Lee Vining

Day 5: Today is one of two days in Yosemite! Beginning with a hike at the Tuolumne Meadows, enjoy a side of Yosemite National Park most visitors don't even know exists. From here head to the Hetch Hetchy Valley, stopping at the Rainbow Pool or hiking to the Tuolumne Grove (sequoias) along the way. Enjoy the easy (but long) hike along the Hetch Hetchy Reservoir with towering granite cliffs and monoliths all around. **Sleep in:** Groveland

Day 6: Start your day early so you can beat the crowds. Today is all about Yosemite Valley. By making stops at Bridalveil Fall, Lower Yosemite Fall, and the Ansel Adams Gallery you'll get the best of the park. For a challenging but unforgettable hike, do the Half Dome trail stopping at Vernal and Nevada Falls. Preregistering for a permit is required to go to the top of Half Dome. When you're done in the valley, head south out of the park, stopping at Tunnel View and the Merced Grove before you leave. **Sleep in:** Oakhurst

Day 7: Kings Canyon National Park is your next stop. Begin at Grant Grove to experience sequoias up close, including walking through the Fallen Monarch (giant hollow tree tunnel). Then move on to Zumwalt Meadows where an easy hike will take you into the valley and you'll be surrounded by Kings Canyon's granite mountains. **Sleep in:** Sequoia National Park

Day 8: Sequoia National Park is fun and fascinating. Start with a stroll through the General Sherman Tree area, followed by the loop through the Giant Forest. Make a reservation for a cave tour so you can explore the Crystal Cave. Finish the day by climbing up Moro Rock for sunset. **Sleep in:** Sequoia National Park

Day 9: Explore just a bit more of Sequoia National Park before you leave. Start with the Tokopah Falls hike out of the Lodgepole area. Then visit the tunnel log, Hospital Rock, and head out to your departure city. **Sleep in:** Fresno or your departure city

Day 10 (optional): There are more hikes in all of these national parks that are truly unique and exciting. Add a day at any of them to dig deeper into each park. And if you're staying at one of the many lodges or ranches outside of the parks, having time to relax and explore the national forests outside the parks is always a good idea.

Depart: Fly out of Fresno (FAT) or out of your initial Bay Area airport

CIRCLING UTAH

You'll see lots of vultures in Utah, circling like they have a plan. Well, here's a plan for you. Utah is a fascinating area with both desolate landscapes and . . . barbeque? This road trip plan will take you through some of the most popular national parks in the US as well as through territory that you might otherwise try to drive through quickly. And be sure to eat local as you explore, because Utah has some great barbeque and local cuisine.

After this road trip through Utah, if somebody asks you why you like the Southwest, you'll have an easy, unarguable answer.

Since so much of this road trip is *extremely* remote, be sure that you're well stocked with backup water (you can never have too much) and lots of snacks. Sometimes it's more than an hour between services, and they may not always be open. Be well prepared for any situation.

Start: Fly into Salt Lake City (SLC) or Las Vegas (LAS). There are flights into Moab (CNY) or Cedar City (CDC) as well, but the amount of time spent changing planes and waiting is better spent driving from a larger airport.

Day 1: Drive from Salt Lake City to Provo, where you can start your adventure immediately by heading up Provo Peak. It's a tough hike but beautiful, but if you're not quite ready for eleven miles at the start of your trip, head to Buffalo Peak instead. Both will get you sweeping views. Continue your drive toward Moab. On the way, you'll have countless opportunities to stop and admire the landscape. If you didn't hike earlier in the day, visit Dead Horse Point State Park or Corona Arch for a taste of what's in store for the rest of your Utah road trip. **Sleep in:** Moab

Day 2: Exploring Arches National Park will definitely wow you. Head into the park early and make your way to the Devils Garden Trailhead. For an active hike, head out to the Double O Arch, coming across plenty of other arches and formations along the way (4.5 miles round-trip). If you still have energy and want to check out one more spectacular area, hike to the Park Avenue Viewpoint (two miles round-trip). Moab has some great restaurants and the town only seems to be growing. Watch for barbeque pits or trucks. **Sleep in:** Moab

Day 3: Today we're going to Canyonlands National Park. Although it's very close to Arches, it's shockingly different. Head toward the Island in the Sky entrance and start at Grand View Point. As you wind your way back toward the entrance, stop at each overlook, and try the short hikes at Mesa Arch and Aztec Butte. **Sleep in:** Moab

Day 4: You'll start by backtracking on the highway a little since Moab was farther south than the loop highway, but that's okay because we're heading to Capitol Reef National Park. While you could spend a week canyoneering and rock climbing, a simple trek onto Scenic Drive with stops at the many viewpoints should satisfy your curiosity. For a beautiful hike, Hickman Bridge or Cohab Canyon will wow you. And easy walks like the Goosenecks Trail and Sunset Point can fill any extra time you have. **Sleep in:** Torrey

Day 5: It's easy to breeze through Grand Staircase–Escalante National Monument, but why would you? Instead, go off the main road a bit and explore Devils Garden. This is a different Devils Garden from the one in Arches. Here, you can climb between hoodoos (stone chimney-like formations) and natural bridges, enjoying the natural playground of Escalante. Also, the small town of Escalante has a few small restaurants, so this is another great place to see what the rural Utah food scene has to offer. When you head back out to the main highway, plan to stop at Escalante Petrified Forest State Park to hike the Trail of Sleeping Rainbows. Finish out the day by watching the shadows grow in Kodachrome Basin State Park. This day of views and hikes may be my favorite in all Utah. **Sleep in:** Tropic or Bryce

Day 6: Spend the day hiking in Bryce Canyon National Park enjoying the Queens Garden and Navajo Trails. You might also choose to do the Rim Trail and then ride the shuttle back to the Visitors Center. You'll have lots of amazing views, but will want to keep an eye on the time. Hiking in Bryce Canyon can be dangerous in the dark. **Sleep in:** Tropic or Bryce

Day 7: You'll get one more day of hiking in Bryce Canyon before you move on. The Peek-A-Boo Loop Trail is longer and brings you to some strange sights you definitely haven't seen before. When you're done, drive through Dixie National Forest, where sandstone arches make tunnels as you exit Bryce. If you like, stop at the Thunder Mountain Trail (no, not Disneyland) and see where the inspiration for the famous roller coaster came from. Enjoy the sunset views in Zion National Park as you rest up and prepare for tomorrow. **Sleep in:** Springdale

Day 8: Get up early to beat the crowds for your day of hiking in Zion National Park. You can either ride the shuttle to the end of the canyon or hike the Pa'rus Trail and ride back. You can also use the shuttle to visit the main sights, after which you head to the Canyon Overlook or Angels Landing trails. Angels Landing is longer and more difficult, so only start it if you know you can safely finish before dark. **Sleep in:** Springdale

Day 9: Visit Snow Canyon State Park for a different sort of hiking day, with volcanic areas and striking colors. Enjoy the scenery and then hike the Lava Tube Trail, where you'll find red sandstone, black lava, cholla cacti and colors you haven't seen in your previous park visits. When you're done, head north for one final visit to Zion National Park at the Kolob Canyons. Very different from the Zion Valley, Kolob is dramatic with the Timber Creek Overlook Trail being short yet breathtaking. If you have more time, hit the Lee Pass Trail, but be sure to be back to your car before sunset. **Sleep in:** Cedar City

Day 10: This is the end of your trip. Today you need to drive back to Salt Lake City, stopping at Cedar Breaks National Monument for one last epic view, or you can relax in Cedar City, enjoying the town and recuperating from an amazing ten days in Utah.

Depart: Fly out of Cedar City (CDC) if you can return your car there; otherwise head back to Salt Lake City (SLC) or Las Vegas (LAS). Since this road trip route is a loop, you can start from any point, whichever is closest to your arrival airport.

Happy hiking!

SOUTHERN WISCONSIN

Wisconsin is known for its dairy industry and Door County, and rightly so. This road trip plan is anything but that, but it's just as fun and memorable. Take a moment and be flexible with your travel ideas: Have you ever considered Wisconsin for a road trip or vacation?

Well, now is your chance to be convinced. I know this road trip route, featuring nature, breweries, and metropolitan fun, will have you ready to fly into Wisconsin and set off on a midwestern adventure! **Tip:** Try fried cheese curds or beer chips at every opportunity you can. Wisconsin has wonderful local food options. Make sure to visit vintage steakhouses too, because a Wisconsin relish plate is a must.

Start: You can fly into either Milwaukee (MKE) or Madison (MSN) from most major US hubs but expect a layover if you're flying from the South or California (don't worry there are many flight options). Whichever airport you choose, you'll want to spend your first night in Milwaukee so you can hit the ground running on day one. **Sleep in:** Milwaukee

Day 1: Waking up in Milwaukee, this is a day to explore a really industrial and yet very metropolitan city. With museums like Discovery World, the Milwaukee Art Museum, and Milwaukee Public Museum, you'll have plenty to do on either hot or rainy days. One of the most unique activities in downtown Milwaukee is actually kayaking through the city. Wander through the Historic Third Ward district and the Riverwalk for a great understanding of the city's history and brewing culture. **Sleep in:** Milwaukee

Day 2: Grab breakfast in the Murray Hill neighborhood and then check out Black Cat Alley, an incredible public art and mural area. As you head out of town, make a stop at the Mitchell Park Horticultural Conservatory. Drive toward Oconomowoc for lunch and to see the enormous historic homes on Lake Road before spending an afternoon kayaking on the Oconomowoc River, launching from Upper Oconomowoc Lake. When you're done, head into Madison where you'll have a few days to explore. If you arrive early enough, go kayaking on Lake Wingra and explore the vast spreads of lily pads. **Sleep in:** Madison

Day 3: Have fun exploring downtown Madison, including the capitol building and Museum of Contemporary Art. Madison is full of breweries with great outdoor seating, so enjoy the local craft beers and, of course, fried cheese curds. After lunch head over to the Olbrich Botanical Gardens to enjoy one of the prettiest established gardens in the Midwest. Finish the afternoon at Hudson Park on Lake Monona and stay for sunset if you can. Eat dinner downtown and you're set for the night. **Sleep in:** Madison

Day 4: Get ready for a day in Wisconsin's beautiful outdoors . . . and underground. Begin your day by heading to Cave of the Mounds to tour a surprisingly cool underground cavern system. Have lunch in Mount Horeb, the troll capital of Wisconsin, and then head north to Devil's Lake State Park. Pick a few short hikes to enjoy, including Devil's Doorway, Parfrey's Glen, and the West Bluff Trails. If you have time, head over to Natural Bridge State Park for one more hike before grabbing dinner in Sauk City. **Sleep in:** Madison

Day 5: Leaving the Madison area and heading toward Lake Michigan, it's time to enjoy farm country. On the way to Lake Geneva, stop by an orchard or farm stand to either pick your own fruit or support the locals. Stop in Williams Bay for some kayaking on Lake Geneva before you get into the actual townsite. Have a picnic lunch along the Lake Geneva Shore Path as you enjoy public art and historic mansions overlooking the lake. When you're done, hop in the car and head for Kenosha. Have dinner looking across Lake Michigan and be ready for an early start tomorrow. **Sleep in:** Kenosha

Day 6: Begin the day with a walk along Lake Michigan and visit the Southport Light Station, Kenosha Lighthouse, and the Kenosha Sand Dunes. After you've had a relaxing morning by the water, pop over to the Dinosaur Discovery Museum (a must with kids) or the Kenosha Public Museum, followed by lunch downtown. If you're inspired, the Jelly Belly Factory is nearby and you can tour it if that sounds fun. Either have dinner in downtown Kenosha or head north to Racine. Up in Racine is the Wind Point Lighthouse, which is beautiful and a must to cross off your lighthouse bucket list (if you're like me). **Sleep in:** Kenosha

Depart: Head back to your starting point to fly home. If you would like to add on to this road trip through Wisconsin, take another three days and make your way up to Door County. The rugged shorelines and lighthouses will be worth it.

DITCHING DENVER

Don't get me wrong, I love Denver. It's historic, it has an amazing food scene, and is full of so much art! But let's just for a moment plan to leave the city and do a loop around western Colorado. Landscapes that rival Utah, mountain towns that make you forget the ocean, and people that are proud of their state make a trip out of Denver a can't-miss road trip.

As you travel through Colorado, keep in mind that this state is known for its bizarre weather. I've enjoyed 85-degree hiking adventures and then woken up to snow the next day. Be prepared for all weather as you head out to explore beyond Denver.

Start: Fly into Denver (DEN). Because it's a major hub, you can get a

direct flight to DEN from nearly anywhere in the US or a major Canadian city. Spend your first night in Denver or Morrison.

Day 1: Start your day with some easy but beautiful hiking at Red Rocks Park. The sandstone is gorgeous, and the wildlife is abundant. From there, head to Dinosaur Ridge for some more easy hiking to see fossilized footprints, dinosaur bones still in the hillside, and an in-process (halted) dinosaur dig. Enjoy lunch at Red Rocks or in nearby Morrison before heading to Lair o' the Bear Park for a bit more nature and footbridges, including views of rocky gorges and out across the region. **Sleep in:** Boulder

Day 2: Wake up in Boulder and explore the town, finding breakfast on Pearl Street. Check out the Museum of Boulder and then take a bike ride along the creek trail. As you head out of town, plan a short hike at the Flatiron rock formations. From there, drive toward Estes Park. Here you've got another beautiful downtown to wander through. Enjoy some Colorado barbecue for dinner and watch the elk wander through town. **Sleep in:** Estes Park

Day 3: Head into Rocky Mountain National Park. You can either guide yourself or do a jeep tour but be sure to check out Alberta Falls and the Cub Lake Trail. Enjoy another evening in Estes Park, walking along the river and trying to find the many bronze pikas that are installed all through the town. **Sleep in:** Estes Park

Day 4: Ideally, you'll be able to drive through Rocky Mountain National Park to the western exit, but if it's closed due to snow, you'll just need to plan a little extra drive time to get to Hot Sulphur Springs. Grab lunch, visit the pioneer cemetery, and then head into the Arapaho and Roosevelt National Forests. Here you can hike along the Continental Divide, watch for wildlife, or if you're timing is right, enjoy the best of Colorado leaf peeping. End this day in Eagle, and enjoy the Old West facades and lodging. **Sleep in:** Eagle

Day 5: Today you visit one of the least talked about national parks: Black Canyon of the Gunnison. You'll want to have packed a picnic lunch for the day. Start with the South Rim Road scenic drive, stopping at overlooks and for short hikes. From here, head to East Portal Road for more exploring and epic views. As you leave, you'll get a chance to experience a bit of Curecanti National Recreation Area. Expect to end your day late, as you'll want to make many stops along the way for views and historic sites. **Sleep in:** Gunnison

Day 6: Heading toward Pikes Peak, today includes some really cool Old West towns, but the first stop is at the Monarch Crest to take the scenic tramway up the mountain. Plan for some hiking at the top, or just enjoy the views and head back down. On your drive, take a short detour to check out the Royal Gorge Bridge and Park (a big wow). From here, make your way to the Old West mining town of Victor for the Vindicator Valley Trail mine loop, which may seem a bit haunted. Continue on to Cripple Creek to enjoy a late lunch and some mining history. End your day by exploring Florissant Fossil Beds National Monument, which includes stargazing! **Sleep in:** Woodland Park

Day 7: This is the last day of exploring and it's really amazing with very little driving (and it's a picnic day too). Begin by heading to the Pikes Peak Cog Railway to ride up the mountain. When you're done, very nearby are the Manitou Cliff Dwellings, which will leave you in awe of time and history. Explore the many rock formations and trail systems in the Garden of the Gods and pay a visit to the nature center at the park if you have time. Finish your day at Broadmoor Seven Falls to hike through a waterfall-filled gorge. Enjoy dinner in Old Colorado City, where you'll also spend the night. **Sleep in:** Old Colorado City or Colorado Springs in general

Depart: Drive back to Denver International Airport (DEN) or continue to explore Colorado further. By now you've gotten to see how diverse and beautiful Colorado is and you may want to continue on, visiting Durango, Great Sand Dunes National Park, and more!

OVERLOOKED TEXAS

When people think of Texas, they usually think about Austin. Austin food, Austin art . . . But this trip will instead take you through parts of Texas you didn't know you'd love. Yes, of course there's barbecue and ranches, but there is definitely more that you're not expecting.

As with any itinerary, adjust it to your likes and the weather. Exploring Texas is fun, but it can be very hot. Be well prepared for scorching temperatures but also thunderstorms. Remember, everything's bigger in Texas.

Start: Fly into Amarillo (AMA), making your connection in either Dallas, Houston, Denver, or Las Vegas. It's a small airport, but with flights from major hubs, it isn't difficult to get to. **Sleep in:** Amarillo

Day 1: Exploring the Amarillo area is fun and funny, with roadside signs and sights that are truly Texan. This is ranch country, so start out with a steak breakfast (you *are* in Texas) and then head to Cadillac Ranch, which is a funky art installation off the highway. From here, head to Wildcat Bluff Nature Center for a short hike in the Texas high desert before it gets too hot. Next, head to the nearby Amarillo Botanical Gardens to see beautiful plants and flowers from around the world, including a conservatory. Grab some local barbecue for lunch, and then head out of town to the Kwahadi Museum of the American Indian. Wrap up your day in Amarillo with dinner at the iconic Big Texan Steak Ranch. Good luck with their steak challenge. **Sleep in:** Amarillo

Day 2: Time to explore the fascinating geology and nature of Texas!

Head out early to start your day with a scenic drive and hike at Palo Duro Canyon State Park, the Grand Canyon of Texas. Hike the Lighthouse or Juniper Cliffside Trails for some exercise and amazing views followed by driving to the end of the loop and back. Grab lunch in either Canyon or Happy (yes, there is a "Happy Cemetery") and then visit Caprock Canyons State Park. Known for its bison and bats, there is plenty of nature to captivate you. Hiking options include the Clarity Tunnel and Canyon Rim Trail. Stay away from the bison but enjoy watching and listening to them. **Sleep in:** Matador

Day 3: A very Texas day awaits by starting with an early ranch day in Matador. After a morning ride, head to Copper Breaks State Park for a little hiking and watching for wild Texas longhorns. If you're traveling with your own kayak or SUP (stand-up paddleboard), go out on the lake (wake free) and enjoy the scenery being surrounded by the caprock breaks. Head out and grab lunch in Stamford before you get to Buffalo Gap in Abilene. The Taylor County History Center is a great stop and walking around the historic village will be a nice change after two days of desert hiking. **Sleep in:** Abilene

Day 4: Wake up and walk around downtown Abilene before heading off to Mineral Wells Fossil Park. This is a really special place, even though by the looks of it, it's not much. Here you can dig for and collect your own fossils, as this was the site of a massive land dump that contained countless fossils. And you can take them! Your next stop is Lake Mineral Wells State Park. Bring your picnic basket and enjoy some easy hiking or rent a kayak to paddle around the beautiful rocky outcroppings of the lake. When you're done, head to Granbury to enjoy a lush, small town with B&Bs and live music. **Sleep in:** Granbury

Day 5: Enjoy your morning walking along the Brazos River in the town of Granbury before you head to Dinosaur Valley State Park. Here, you can spot dinosaur tracks, learn about prehistoric Texas, and go horseback riding through the valley. In the afternoon head to Killeen for lunch and to play at the lake. Chalk Ridge Falls flows into Stillhouse Hollow Lake and

is the perfect spot to relax after a day of dinosaurs and horseback riding.
Sleep in: Killeen

Day 6: Killeen is just north of Texas Hill Country wine region. Before you head to Dallas to end your road trip through Texas, be sure to plan a day of wine tasting and great food from Killeen to Cedar Park to Granite Shoals. End your day out with a stop at Cedar Breaks Park on Georgetown Lake, checking out the weeping bluff (cliffside with flowing water) of Crockett Gardens Falls and taking a dip in the lake. **Sleep in:** Killeen

Depart: After seeing so much of the Texas countryside, arriving in Dallas is going to feel like you've been wandering in the desert for weeks. Fly out of Dallas (DFW or DAL), or spend a few days playing tourist or eating Texas BBQ and Tex-Mex. This trip has been a side of Texas most people don't see, so be sure to share your adventures with everyone you meet who would have never explored beyond the city.

FLORIDA GULF COAST

Yes, Florida has two coasts: the Gulf and the Atlantic. And yes, they are very different. The Florida Gulf Coast is all about beaches. Seriously, you can visit a different beach every day, and they all vary in sand type and shells. True, you're not going to be surfing a whole lot, but you'll be laughing with dolphins, beachcombing, and eating Greek food (just wait for Tarpon Springs!). You can't go wrong. Oh, and there are manatees.

This particular trip begins in Miami and heads north, but you can also do it in reverse, starting in Tampa and heading south. Whichever way you choose, you're sure to see some remarkable wildlife and get your fill of sand between your toes.

Start: Fly into Miami (MIA) or Fort Lauderdale (FLL). If you have time on this first day, explore 8th Street/Calle Ocho or head to Biscayne National Park for a boat tour. This day can also be spent putting together your road trip vehicle with shopping and organizing, as there are lots of picnic days ahead.

Day 1: Depart Miami nice and early. Your first stop is Everglades National Park in the Shark Valley area. Here, you can either bike or take the tram deep into the glades, watching for alligators, turtles, and even manatees. Climb the observation tower and take in the vastness of Florida's grass islands. Head out from Shark Valley to Big Cypress National Preserve. Stop at the Oasis Visitor Center for hiking recommendations on the boardwalks of the swamp, as weather may make some trails flood. End your day with sunset on Tigertail Beach on Marco Island. **Sleep in:** Marco Island

Day 2: Begin the day by heading up to Naples Beach for breakfast. Take a walk on the pier to watch for dolphins or stroll on the beach. When you're ready, head north to Fort Myers Beach. Stop at Lovers Key State Park for kayaking through the mangroves and to the beach, enjoying a picnic on the sand. After kayaking, continue north to Sanibel where you can visit the lighthouse and walk the perfect beaches, visit the Bailey-Matthews National Shell Museum, and then end your day watching another perfect sunset on the Gulf of Mexico. **Sleep in:** Sanibel Island

Day 3: If finding shark teeth is on your Gulf Coast bucket list, today is the day. Grab breakfast to go and drive to Venice. Caspersen Beach is known as one of the best shark tooth hunting beaches on the gulf and it stretches for miles. When you've found your fill, walk around downtown Venice and seek out a nice patio for lunch. Next stop is either a relaxing beach afternoon at Bradenton Beach or exploring the Little Manatee River via kayak or SUP. Let your mood guide you. **Sleep in:** Bradenton

Day 4: Today begins by crossing one of the most spectacular bridges in Florida: the Sunshine Skyway Bridge. After crossing the bridge, your first destination is Fort De Soto State Park to explore the bunkers, enjoy the beach, and spend the morning birdwatching. Once you've had your fill of perfect, shelly sand, head to the Salvador Dalí Museum in St. Pete for a slice of culture and then eat lunch at the museum. Visit St. Pete Beach for a different side of Florida life, including a high-class evening at the Don CeSar Hotel. Even if you don't stay overnight, this is vintage Florida you cannot find anywhere else. **Sleep in:** St. Pete Beach

Day 5: Clearwater is your next stop. Many say the beaches of Clearwater are the best in Florida, so you need to invest some time confirming this. You'll also find the Clearwater Marine Aquarium here, which is a must with kids. Wind out the afternoon with biking and exploring the forest at Honeymoon Island State Park. Keeping the driving to a minimum, you'll finish the day in Tarpon Springs, the most fascinating Greek settlement on the Gulf Coast. **Sleep in:** Tarpon Springs

Day 6: Start the morning with a stroll along the sponge docks of Tarpon Springs and a hearty Greek breakfast. If you need some beach time, go early out to Fred Howard Park, but keep an eye on the time so you can make it to Weeki Wachee Springs State Park. Here, you can see mermaids (you read that correctly), swim at a gorgeous freshwater spring, and do clear kayaks on the river. A picnic is good if you're planning on spending all day here. When you're ready, drive up to Rainbow Springs State Park for one more taste of freshwater springs paradise. Have a dip in the springs, wander through the abandoned zoo, and enjoy the man-made waterfalls. **Sleep in:** Crystal River

Day 7: Wake up early to go snorkeling with manatees. Don a wetsuit and head out with a guide for the unique experience of being in the water with enormous manatees (go as early as possible). When you're done, visit Three Sisters Springs to walk the boardwalks and enjoy the turquoise scenery. Relax at Hunter Springs with some swimming or rent kayaks to explore. Feel free to pop down to Homosassa Springs Wildlife State Park if you feel like you need one more experience, as it's very different and actually has a Florida wildlife zoo and an underwater viewing room for getting closer to the springs. **Sleep in:** Crystal River

Day 8: Today is the final day of exploring and also takes you back to

your starting location. Your drive time will be just over five hours, so there are a few easy stops to break it up. As you head back to Miami, stop in Ybor City for a Cuban sandwich in the wrought iron balconied historic district. As you make your way south, feel free to go the shortest route or drive through Big Cypress Preserve one more time, stopping at Big Bend or any of the Everglades areas you missed the first time.

Sleep in: Miami

Depart: You can fly out of either Miami (MIA) or Fort Lauderdale (FLL). A bonus you can add if time allows is the Florida Keys. While four or five days is ideal for touring the Keys, you can add just a day or two and get a good idea of what lies to the south for your next Florida road trip.

NORTHEAST FLORIDA: WHERE NATURE MEETS HISTORY

Indeed, there are two Florida road trips that you *must* do. Northeast Florida is a special region and one of the most overlooked when it comes to vacation destinations. From Jacksonville to NASA and then inland, the First Coast includes everything you could dream of.

If you ever wanted to spend your week walking the walls of an almost five-hundred-year-old city, smell the breath of dolphins as you kayak, and then park yourself on the beach to watch a rocket launch, this is the trip for you.

Start: Fly into Orlando (MCO) and head for the beach. Unless you're flying from Eastern Standard Time, your arrival will probably be after 4:00 p.m. and you won't have time to explore Orlando much, so make your way to the coast if you don't mind the hourlong drive after flying. You can either spend this first night in Orlando (late arrival) or head to Cocoa Beach (earlier arrival).

Day 1: Let yourself get used to the Florida vibe and new time zone (if you came from the west). Spend the day relaxing on the beach and enjoying the town. Walk around looking for marine-themed murals and enjoy the many outdoor dining experiences. Have lunch on the beach and dinner over the water on the Intracoastal Waterway. **Sleep in:** Cocoa Beach

Day 2: Explore the Space Coast with a visit to Cape Canaveral and Kennedy Space Center, and if you're lucky, watch a rocket launch. Visit Titusville on the Indian River (Intracoastal Waterway) and watch for manatees in one of their favorite places to congregate, the Merritt Island National Wildlife Refuge. Have some afternoon beach time at Playalinda and then head back into Titusville for dinner. End your day with bio-luminescent kayaking on Mosquito Lagoon, as dolphins, manatees, and even alligators glow in the water all around you (May–October). **Sleep in:** Cocoa Beach

Day 3: Head north to Daytona Beach. It's much more than the spring break destination you might think of. Visit the Ponce de Leon Inlet Lighthouse and Museum and Marine Science Center then enjoy some of the most beautiful turquoise waters in Florida, either at the mouth of the inlet or any of the beach access points along Florida A1A. In the evening, head to the famous Daytona Beach Boardwalk and Pier for people watching and dinner on the oceanfront. **Sleep in:** Flagler Beach

Day 4: Wake up to walk the beach at sunrise and relax as long as you like. Rent kayaks and explore the Intracoastal Waterway and grass islands at North Peninsula or Gamble Rogers Memorial State Park. Have an authentic North Florida lunch in Flagler Beach with either a blackened or grilled fish sandwich. Washington Oaks Gardens is a perfect stop along the way, with beautiful subtropical botanical gardens and astounding live oaks covered in Spanish moss. Continue north to St. Augustine, the oldest city in the United States. Visit the Castillo de San Marcos National Monument just before it closes, and then walk through the historic downtown. Its piratey-Caribbean-meets-colonial-America feel will make you fall in love with the city. **Sleep in:** St. Augustine

Day 5: Today is all about shark teeth, history, and amazing food. Begin your day walking through the historic narrow streets of downtown St. Augustine, where you'll find coffee and biscuits to fill you up. Then, head north to drive down Magnolia Avenue, the "most beautiful street in the United States" per *National Geographic* on your way to the GTM Research Reserve Middle Beach. Here, you'll enjoy watching for dolphins and pelicans as well as hunting for shark teeth. This stretch of beach between Vilano and Jacksonville is known for finding fossils, including shark teeth. When you're ready, head back to downtown St. Augustine to wander the streets and find dinner. Be sure to go past Flagler College and the Lightner Museum to appreciate some of the incredible architecture of the city.

Sleep in: St. Augustine

Day 6: Say goodbye to the beach as you head to see a completely different side of Florida. After one last stroll in downtown St. Augustine, make your way to Ravine Gardens State Park for some of the only hiking in Northeast Florida. After a quick stop in the historic town of Palatka to grab coffee for the road, you'll arrive at Silver Springs State Park. The Silver River is known for its history in the film industry, from James Bond movies to *Creature from the Black Lagoon*. Either do a glass bottom boat tour to spy on manatees and fish or rent kayaks to explore on your own. There are many alligators and even monkeys along the Silver River, so proceed with caution. In the evening, walk through historic Ocala to seek out dinner.

Sleep in: Ocala

Day 7: I save the best for last. Today is all about Florida's freshwater springs. Begin your day at Alexander Springs Recreation Area, where you can swim over one of the most beautiful bubbling springs. Paddleboard or kayak down the river a bit to see countless turtles, alligators, ibises, and even more springs bubbling in the middle of the river. Next stop is De Leon Springs State Park. Have lunch at the historic Old Spanish Sugar Mill and then take a dip in the gorgeous De Leon Springs. Head to Blue Spring State Park next. In the winter months, hundreds of manatees congregate here below the viewing platforms; in spring through fall, it's perfect for swimming. Wrap up your day of exploring with a quick visit to Gemini Springs Park. Here, you'll walk through enormous live oaks to two pristine springs. Watch for alligators as you make your way to the subtropical forest path to stroll through a wild orange grove. Get dinner in DeBary. **Sleep in:** DeBary

Depart: Fly out of Orlando (MCO) or continue over to the Gulf Coast. You'll find a very different world on that side of Florida and you'll enjoy it just as much.

HISTORIC VIRGINIA AND DC

I love this road trip route for many reasons. I remember doing it as a kid and I've since gotten to relive this road trip with my own children. There's something about being able to see the places you've learned about in school, or be able to explain to kids that "This is where . . ."

For my family, this trip was really fun, and a first-timer trip to the National Capital Region. This was also the first time either of our kids were genuinely interested in history. They even wanted period costumes, but you'll have to decide if that's right for you.

Start: Fly into either Washington Reagan (DCA) or Washington Dulles (IAD), as this is where your loop road trip will end. If you would like to do a straight shot, fly into Newport News (PHF) and then out of a DC area airport. Depending on your origin, Baltimore (BWI) may also be an option instead of DCA or IAD.

Day 1: Drive from the Washington, DC, area south to the Newport News region of Virginia. It's always best to get some beach time to start a vacation, so start with Virginia Beach and begin your road trip with relaxation and fun. There's a boardwalk and wonderful townsite to entertain you. It's the perfect way to start your trip feeling refreshed. **Sleep in:** Virginia Beach

Day 2: After breakfast, make your way to Chippokes Plantation State Park to do some kayaking or tour the antebellum mansion and farm. This is also a place known for finding megalodon shark teeth, so keep your eyes out! Next, visit Bacon's Castle, the oldest brick home in North America, before driving onto the very small (free) ferry from Scotland to Jamestown. At Jamestown, enjoy the very comprehensive museum detailing the history of the area and then wander through the settlement, including touring the sailing ships. Make a reservation for dinner at the King's Arms Tavern in Colonial Williamsburg for a historical meal by candlelight. **Sleep in:** Williamsburg

Day 3: Immerse yourself in living history with a full day in Colonial Williamsburg. Visiting the Governor's Palace, capitol building, and the many blacksmithing shops, this is a fun day full of unique experiences. If you finish Colonial Williamsburg early, you can drive over to Yorktown to visit the American Revolution Museum and stroll along the Riverwalk. Head back to the town of Williamsburg to find dinner, winding out your day with a ghost tour by candlelight. **Sleep in:** Williamsburg

Day 4: Head north to Westmoreland State Park for exploring more of the coastal marsh area by kayak or look for shark teeth in one of the most concentrated fossil areas in Virginia. Plan a visit to Stratford Hall if you need another living history experience or if you just want to wander the grounds of this amazing estate. After some lunch in Montrose, visit George Washington Birthplace National Monument. Leaving this rural part of Virginia, make your way to Mount Vernon, George Washington's home, for one last historical tour. **Sleep in:** Fairfax or Alexandria

Day 5: Find breakfast in town before you head north to Great Falls Park, where you'll walk along the raging, epic rapids of the Potomac. Your next stop is the Udvar-Hazy Center, the Smithsonian National Air and Space Museum's annex. Here you'll get to see all kinds of aircrafts and even a space shuttle! Head to downtown Alexandria to wander around Old Town and the waterfront, eventually getting dinner in the historic quarter. **Sleep in:** Fairfax or Alexandria

Day 6/7: The next day or two is spent exploring Washington, DC, the nation's capital. You no longer need a car as you can take the Metro wherever you need to go, including back to the airport (DCA, IAD, BWI). Visit the greatest museums in the USA as you spend time in the many Smithsonian museums. Top choices:

- Museum of Natural History
- Museum of American History
- Museum of African American History and Culture
- Museum of the American Indian
- American Art Museum
- National Portrait Gallery

This is a lot of museums, so pace yourself and know that you don't have to do or see them all.

In addition to the museums, there are also fascinating sights and tours to do, including Ford's Theater, the Capitol, and the Washington Monument. Visit the United States Botanic Garden, walk the National Mall, and make your way to the Tidal Basin and the Jefferson Memorial. To do it all, you need three or four days, but two days is plenty if you choose what's most important to you. **Sleep in:** Either continue where you've been staying or switch to a hotel in DC.

Depart: Take the train to your departure airport. If you're continuing to explore the National Capital Region, it's easy to head north into Maryland or New Jersey, and Philadelphia is also fairly close and an easy addition to your road trip.

NYC TO THE FINGER LAKES

New York City may not be a road trip destination, but it's a great starting point. New York State is so much more than the Big Apple, and this road trip plan gives you a tremendously broad perspective. From the Hudson

Valley to Finger Lakes Wine Country (and National Votes for Women Trail), you'll experience history, nature, and culture unlike anything you thought a road trip could provide.

Keep in mind that depending on how much you're loving each stop, you can adjust the daily itinerary. There are lots of beautiful towns and unique hikes in this itinerary, so as you get into your upstate NY groove, adapt the plan to fit your realistic schedule.

Start: Fly into New York City (JFK or LGA) or Newark (EWR) to begin your trip. If you would like to have a few days exploring NYC, do it at the start of your trip, as the quiet of upstate NY will be even more of a refreshing calm after touring the City That Never Sleeps.

Day 1: If you spent the night in NYC, get up early and head out of Manhattan up to Sleepy Hollow. There are many charming towns in the Hudson Valley, but Sleepy Hollow is a must stop (if for nothing else than to just say that you looked for the Headless Horseman). Next up, head to Poughkeepsie for lunch before visiting the Walkway Over the Hudson. Cross the river if you like, or just enjoy the view. Next stop is touring the Vanderbilt Mansion National Historic Site, a fascinating insight into high-class life during the empire days. End your day in Kingston, one of the most quaint, charming towns you'll come across. **Sleep in:** Kingston

Day 2: Wake up and go for a stroll around Kingston if you didn't get to the night before. After some breakfast in the historic town, head up to the village of Catskill, where the story of Rip Van Winkle is set. Walk Main Street and support the locals running the many shops before you make your way to the Mohonk Labyrinth for a hike that will drop your jaw. After, meander up to Kaaterskill Falls, the tallest cascading waterfall in New York. It's an easy hike, or you can even view it from your car if you like. Head toward Ithaca, making stops at Delaware Wild Forest to hike Tompkins Falls. Drive across the Beaverkill Bridge and then up to Downsville. Spend the afternoon kayaking and enjoying the countryside. **Sleep in:** Sidney or Bainbridge

Day 3: Enjoy the short drive to Ithaca, where you'll have lots of time to explore the picturesque town. While here, take advantage of the access to nature with easy hikes and strolls along the Cascadilla Gorge Trail, nearby Buttermilk Falls State Park, and the Ithaca Falls Natural Area. For a beautiful afternoon, be sure to visit the Cornell Botanic Gardens before sunset. Enjoy an evening downtown with local chefs and a wine tasting characteristic of the Finger Lakes region. **Sleep in:** Ithaca

Day 4: Grab some breakfast and hop in the car. Today you'll experience deep-cut waterfall gorges you didn't know could be real. Your first stop is at Watkins Glen State Park, where nineteen waterfalls will leave you speechless. Head east to get lunch in Montour Falls and take in the view of Shequaga Falls. Finish your day diving into nature with an afternoon hike at Robert H. Treman State Park. Similar to Watkins Glen, you'll love the calm of the flowing streams in the forest. Enjoy one more night in Ithaca. **Sleep in:** Ithaca

Day 5: It's a quick drive over to Corning, where you'll enjoy the art and culture of the Finger Lakes region. Start at the Corning Museum of Glass, where you'll be wowed by the pieces and installations, as well as by the artisans working there. Have a nice lunch downtown enjoying fresh-from-the-farm local produce and wine. Once you're done eating, make sure to visit the Rockwell Museum with its remarkable collection of American art (it's also a Smithsonian affiliate museum). When you're done, stroll along the river, visit a brewery, and enjoy the quiet nature of Corning. **Sleep in:** Corning

Day 6: Have your parting moments with Corning before you head north. You'll see that you're driving through farm country, so be sure to stop and get produce from an honor system roadside stand along your drive (leave money for your purchase in a jar). Your first detour is through Letchworth State Park. Known as the Grand Canyon of the East, the views, easy hikes, and beautiful, gushing waterfall make it the perfect place to picnic. Continue north to Genesee Country Village, where you can enjoy living history and relax in a beautiful farm village setting. Arrive in Rochester in the early evening, enjoying dinner downtown, preferably near High Falls to sneak a peek during the golden hour. **Sleep in:** Rochester

Alternative Day 6: Head up along the western edge of Seneca Lake,

making as many winery stops as you can (since you're in the heart of Finger Lakes Wine Country). Enjoy lunch in Seneca Falls and then dig into history at Women's Rights National Historical Park. Visit the National Women's Hall of Fame, pay homage to some pioneers, and then make your way west. Stop for dinner in Palmyra before you end your day in Rochester.
Sleep in: Rochester

Day 7: Today you get to take in as much of Rochester as you can. Downtown is fun and full of good food, but if you can be there on a farmers' market day (Tue/Thu/Sat), that's the best! After exploring downtown or the market a bit, pop into the Strong National Museum of Play. As an adult, you'll *love* it and be swept back in time, including onto Sesame Street. After a food truck lunch, make your way to Pittsford for a relaxing cruise on the Erie Canal through locks and drooping trees. Finish with an evening downtown enjoying the river, listening to live music of the Eastman School, and falling in love with the city. **Sleep in:** Rochester

Depart: Fly out of Rochester (ROC). While there aren't a ton of direct flights out of ROC, you'll be able to get back to your home airport most likely with one layover. If you have the time or if you need to return your rental car to NYC, you can easily condense Day 6 and make the drive back in the afternoon on Day 7 (but you won't want to, because Rochester is an amazing city). Do what's best for your schedule and enjoy every moment exploring New York!

FIVE CLEARLY CANADIAN ROAD TRIPS

Even though Canada and the United States border each other and are very similar in many ways, the traveling experience in each is very different. This collection of road trips in Canada showcases both the culture and natural beauty of Canada.

From the Maritime Provinces on the east coast, to circling Vancouver Island in the Pacific, these road trip itineraries are ideal for anyone looking to explore Canada, eat amazing food, and enjoy some of the most epic scenery in North America.

In these Canadian road trip itineraries, you'll find:

- Nova Scotia: The Lighthouse Route and Beyond
- French Canada: Ottawa to Québec City
- Nature in Ontario: Niagara to Tobermory
- Best of the Canadian Rockies
- The Vancouver Island Loop

Before planning a trip to Canada, be sure you have the proper documents to cross the border, either via land, air, or sea. Also, make sure you notify your banking institutions that you're traveling across the border.

One last thing to double-check is your auto and health insurance. Be sure of how to use your insurance while in Canada. You may need to add coverage or adjust your mileage declarations, and for health care you may actually need to purchase separate medical coverage.

Online research or a few phone calls with your providers should answer all questions and have you set up for success in case of an emergency. Enjoy the adventure and be safe!

NOVA SCOTIA: THE LIGHTHOUSE ROUTE AND BEYOND

If Nova Scotia wasn't on your road trip bucket list already, 1) Why not? and 2) It definitely should be now. Many people overlook Canada's Maritime Provinces when they're considering travel and road trip destinations, but this area of the world is truly remarkable.

With colorful fishing villages, phenomena of nature that will stun you, and locally caught and farmed food to rival any five-star sustainable restaurant in San Francisco, Nova Scotia is a dream trip. This itinerary covers the western half of the province with options to head east. Plan at least five days and then add more if you can!

This itinerary can easily be done in reverse, so just flip the schedule and you're set. If you're planning this trip as a leaf-peeping adventure in the fall, keep an eye on the weather before your travel dates, as sometimes peak color is a week or two earlier than the prior year. Also, many small-town restaurants and lodgings close down after the first week of October, so plan accordingly.

Start: Fly into Halifax, NS (YHZ). It's likely that you'll have at least one connecting flight, particularly if coming from the US. When you arrive, get situated in your hotel for the night and then seek out dinner downtown or in Dartmouth. **Sleep in:** Halifax or Dartmouth

Day 1: The best way to start a road trip around Nova Scotia is to begin in Halifax. It's a small but very modern city with many museums. The Maritime Museum of the Atlantic is the only one that is truly a must-visit, but the others, including the Discovery Centre and the Natural History Museum, are great options if the weather is bad. Enjoy lunch at the Seaport Farmers' Market and then head up the hill to the Halifax Citadel. Wind up the day walking around downtown, including the Halifax Public Gardens. **Sleep in:** Halifax or Dartmouth

Day 2: Start your day early and head out for a stroll along the canal systems of Shubie Park, which are at their most beautiful when the fall leaves are changing. Then head southeast toward Eastern Passage, stopping at McCormacks Beach Provincial Park to watch for seals and seabirds and perhaps do some beachcombing. Grab lunch at Fisherman's Cove, enjoying the multicolored fishing huts and narrow harbor. Have dinner in downtown Dartmouth where you'll find breweries and restaurants showcasing the diverse cuisines of Nova Scotia. **Sleep in:** Halifax or Dartmouth

Note: The Day 2 plan can actually be narrowed down and added to the end of Day 1 if you're pressed for time. You just can't skip the Shubie Canals.

Day 3: Leave the Halifax area and head to the southwest, enjoying the unique Nova Scotia coastline and nature. For a worthwhile detour visit Duncan's Cove Nature Reserve and Sambro Harbour. On the way to your first planned sight, stop at Polly's Cove Trail to hike (minimal elevation change) to a perfect, unspoiled stretch of coastline. Then move onto Peggy's Cove where Peggy's Point Lighthouse is picture perfect, as is the small fishing village. Grab a lobster roll lunch and then hit the road. Make stops at the many rocky beaches along the way and end your day in the tiny village of Hubbards. It's been a short driving day, so you can go farther if you like, but this is a great stop. **Sleep in:** Hubbards or Mahone Bay

Day 4: Today includes some beautiful sights, so start early with breakfast and a walk around Mahone Bay. Visit Blue Rocks for a morning of kayaking through the rocky coves; it's truly unlike anywhere else. Then head into Lunenburg, a UNESCO World Heritage Site, for a look at a beautifully preserved hillside fishing village. After lunch, explore to the south, visiting Ovens Natural Park and Feltzen South. Drive into Liverpool and have a great dinner of locally caught fish or lobster. **Sleep in:** Liverpool

Note: Days 3 and 4 can actually be combined if you want to go at a faster pace or not make as many stops. Nova Scotia is actually rather small, which makes it easy to cover ground quickly or go very slowly, exploring everything.

Day 5: Grab breakfast and then head to the Fort Point Lighthouse, beautifully set on the inlet. When you're ready, drive to Kejimkujik National Park Seaside, watching for wildlife and whales offshore. Do the Harbour Rocks Trail for an easy hike (5.6 km round-trip) to the coves. Grab lunch in Shelburne before kayaking over to the Islands Provincial Park. From here, head to Yarmouth where you'll find more great local seafood. Take in sunset by the Cape Forchu Lighthouse. **Sleep in:** Yarmouth

Day 6: Leave Yarmouth and head to Kejimkujik National Park (the inland portion), where you'll be able to hike and enjoy the rugged Mersey River. If you'd like to kayak on Kejimkujik Lake there are rentals, or just enjoy the scenery and history. From here, head north to Annapolis Royal to stroll through the picturesque town and grab some lunch. Cross the rainbow crosswalk to the tiny red-and-white lighthouse and enjoy the calm. For some living history and more beautiful views, head across the inlet to Port-Royal National Historic Site. **Sleep in:** Annapolis Royal

Day 7: Today is all about the Bay of Fundy. With the most dramatic tides in the world, there are several stops along the bay to really experience the wonder of nature. Before starting this day, check the tide tables and order these activities to match the tide:

- Hall's Harbour and the Lobster Pound: tide change, high or low
- Black Hole Falls: incoming tide
- Blomidon Provincial Park red beach: low tide

The reason for timing these sights with the tide is so that you can witness the extreme change as dramatically as possible. If you want to go on a hike to experience the raging outgoing tide, hike at Cape Split. It's a long hike at 7.5 miles, but if you have the time and energy and have planned for it, it's phenomenal. **Sleep in:** Halifax or Dartmouth

Depart: Fly out of Halifax (YHZ) when your trip is done. If you like you can even get a lobster to take home while you're at the airport. If you'd like to keep exploring Nova Scotia, head to the eastern cape and enjoy more small towns and the Cape Breton Highlands. Allow yourself an extra two or three days if you add this.

FRENCH CANADA:
OTTAWA TO QUÉBEC CITY

This road trip is as close to a European vacation as you can get without actually being in Europe. Canada has a solid population of French speakers and in some areas hardly anyone speaks English. This mix, paired with an interesting history, makes the trip between Ottawa, the capital, and Québec City a unique road trip.

With a stop in Montréal and several gorgeous natural sites and parks along the way, exploring French Canada is sure to be a memorable journey full of delicious food and beautiful sights.

If you don't speak French and are concerned about this road trip plan through Québec, don't worry. The respectful and kind thing to do is make the effort to communicate in the primary language where you are, and then hope that whomever you're interacting with also speaks your language. Be polite and know that "*s'il vous plaît*" and "*merci*" can go a long way.

Start: Fly into either Québec City (YQB) or Ottawa (YOW). This trip can be done as a one way or a loop. If you're normally based in the northeastern US, you can easily drive to either starting destination in just a few hours from upstate New York, Massachusetts, Vermont, New Hampshire, or Maine. However you choose to arrive, don't forget your passport. **Sleep in:** Ottawa

Day 1: Start your sightseeing road trip by exploring Ottawa, Canada's capital. Visiting the National Gallery, Rideau Hall (the governor general's residence), and the Canadian Museum of Nature are great ideas to start the day. Have lunch in the Vanier neighborhood where you'll hear a mix of French and English in every conversation. After lunch, take a walk along the Rideau Canal on the way to the Notre-Dame Cathedral Basilica. Take in Rideau Falls and enjoy dinner along the canal or Ottawa River. **Sleep in:** Ottawa

Day 2: Enjoy a nice breakfast in Ottawa before leaving the city. The first stop to make after crossing over into Québec is at Parc national de Plaisance (National Park of Pleasure). Here you can explore the beaver lodge marsh and hike to the Chutes de Plaisance (Plaisance Falls). When you're ready, head to the town of Montebello to see the largest log cabin castle in the world (a Fairmont hotel) and have lunch in the charming downtown. Then make your way to Mont-Tremblant National Park. Hike to Chute du

Diable (Diablo Falls) and enjoy the lakes and trails. Have dinner in town and explore on foot after. **Sleep in:** Mont-Tremblant

Day 3: Grab breakfast for the road as you head south to Montréal. Spend the day exploring the old city. Make sure to include the Latin Quarter and Red-Light District, and when you're done, head toward the river for Chinatown and Old Montréal. For lunch, seek out poutine (a must!) and stroll along the historic waterfront. In the afternoon, visit Mount Royal Park overlooking the city, and spend the evening on Saint Laurent Boulevard, where the western side is English-speaking and the eastern side primarily speaks French. **Sleep in:** Montréal

Day 4: Exploring more of the Montréal area, enjoy breakfast in Old Montréal before you head south for the day. Begin with some kayaking and exploring at Îles-de-Boucherville National Park. Before lunch, continue south stopping at Mont-Saint-Bruno National Park to take in the scenery, and then the town of Chambly for lunch. Walk along the historic Chambly Canal and then tour Fort Chambly. Before heading back to Montréal, head east to farm country to visit a cidery or two, bringing some back for the evening. Return to Montréal for dinner near Saint Paul Street and enjoy the city at night. **Sleep in:** Montréal

Day 5: Depart Montréal and head for Mont-Orford National Park to do the Mont-Orford Loop and take in views of the surrounding area. If you prefer, take the gondola from the ski resort for an easier way to explore. When you're done, head south to Parc de la Gorge de Coaticook to cross one of the longest suspension footbridges in the world and visit Foresta Lumina (best at night if you can). As you head north, you're in cider country again, so enjoy stops along the cider route as you end your day in Trois-Rivières. **Sleep in:** Trois-Rivières

Day 6: After breakfast downtown, head to the Moulin à vent de Trois-Rivières to visit a historic mill and farm or stop into the Musée Pierre Boucher downtown. The plan is to explore La Mauricie National Park, stopping at Waber and Parker Falls, but if you would like to do more hiking or see more of the park, just head north right after breakfast. Bring a picnic lunch today. After your hiking and waterfall adventures are done, arrive in Québec City for dinner and an evening of strolling through Old Québec. **Sleep in:** Québec City

Day 7: Enjoy walking around Québec City, including Quartier Petit-Champlain, the citadel, and Notre-Dame de Québec. Visit the historic Château Frontenac and relax in the many parks and squares. Taking in the historic city will fill your day, but if you want one final natural beauty, take a drive out to Montmorency Falls. End the day with one last French-Canadian dinner. **Sleep in:** Québec City

Depart: Fly out of Québec City (YQB) or continue exploring the province. Québec is enormous, and as you continue up the Saint Lawrence River to the Gulf of Saint Lawrence, you'll come across countless colorful towns and history.

Enjoy your time exploring French Canada, and if you didn't get to do everything you wanted, be sure to note those things so you have a plan for next time!

NATURE IN ONTARIO:
NIAGARA FALLS TO TOBERMORY

The province of Ontario reminds me so much of British Columbia: unbelievable waters, striking cliffs and gorges, a major metropolitan city . . . It's beautiful and truly an adventure to explore. This Ontario road trip itinerary stretches from the Canadian side of Niagara Falls to the rugged islands of Tobermory's national parks.

This road trip plan is a loop. There isn't a major airport close to the Bruce Peninsula (Tobermory), so you do need to drive back down south, but luckily there are some beautiful areas and provincial parks to visit, so the loop delivers beautiful sights and nonstop activities (or relaxation).

Due to the remote nature of the Bruce Peninsula, book your stays as far in advance as you're able, because there aren't a ton of options.

Start: Fly into Toronto (YYZ) or Buffalo, NY (BUF). Either is a good option to start this Ontario road trip, but Buffalo may not be a direct flight option for many travelers. This is a great road trip to add onto the NYC to Finger Lakes road trip plan! **Sleep in:** Hamilton, ON

Day 1: Start your Ontario road trip with a bang by visiting the world-famous Niagara Falls. Accessible from both the US and Canadian sides, visit Horseshoe Falls (Canada) and either do a boat tour (and get soaked), or do the Journey Behind the Falls (and stay relatively dry). These are both very touristy activities, but there's a reason people love them. Walk across the Rainbow Bridge to the US side for another view, and then head north on the Canadian side to do the Whitewater Walk. The town of Niagara Falls has all sorts of attractions, but for dinner, head back to Hamilton for a quiet evening. **Sleep in:** Hamilton

Day 2: Grab breakfast in Hamilton as you head to the Royal Botanical Gardens (best in spring). Enjoy the flowers before heading to one of three beautiful natural areas just beyond the town. Visit the Crooks Hollow, Webster's Falls, and Spencer Gorge areas for waterfalls and light hiking (reservation may be required). Make your way south to Albion Falls and the Devil's Punchbowl Conservation area. You'll find that Hamilton is full of natural areas just beyond the neighborhoods. When you're done exploring, grab dinner and relax. **Sleep in:** Hamilton

Day 3: It's time to head to the Bruce Peninsula. Drive to Kincardine, where you'll come to the shores of Lake Huron. Visit the lighthouse and take a walk along the lake before turning north. Stop at Sauble Falls Provincial Park for an easy hike along the terraced cascades. Grab lunch in Sauble Beach or one of the other lakefront towns, and then ultimately arrive in Tobermory. This day is a long drive (4.5 hours), but you can shorten the drive time by only driving north to Tobermory instead of making the suggested stops. **Sleep in:** Tobermory

Day 4: Spend today exploring the turquoise and deep blue waters of Lake Huron at Fathom Five and Bruce Peninsula National Parks. Activities include hiking, swimming, and kayaking around some of the most incredibly clear waters. If you're a diver or a snorkeler, there are more than twenty shipwrecks and countless underwater geological features to explore. And it's all a photographer's dream. **Sleep in:** Tobermory

Day 5: Spend the first half of the day continuing to explore the national parks. Take a boat tour to Flowerpot Island or just relax. Fathom Five National Marine Park is a bucket list paddling destination for many, so if you didn't kayak on day one, that's the perfect use of your time before you leave. Depart Tobermory and head south to Craigleith Provincial Park to enjoy one more perfect part of Lake Huron (again with beautiful turquoise water). Find lunch in the town of Collingwood and pay a visit to the Nottawasaga Lighthouse. Take a walk through the arboretum and continue on to Mono Cliffs Provincial Park. Here you'll find picture-perfect lakes and a staircase/boardwalk system to lead you up through the forest. **Sleep in:** Brampton

Day 6: You're so close to Toronto that you just have to have a day exploring the city. A major metropolitan center, Toronto has a very diverse food and art scene, as well as world-class museums. Visit the Allan Gardens, Hockey Hall of Fame, the Distillery District, Little Italy . . . Really, Toronto could be a four-day trip in itself, so choose a few activities or neighborhood to enjoy. **Sleep in:** Toronto

Depart: Fly out of Toronto (YYZ) or drive back down to Buffalo (BUF) to depart. If you do want more time in Toronto, stick around and enjoy the many sights. You won't need a vehicle unless you want to drive out of the city, so take advantage of public transportation.

Have fun exploring Ontario. It's truly a wonder!

BEST OF THE CANADIAN ROCKIES

Let me start by saying that there is more to the Canadian Rockies than just Banff. Don't get me wrong, Banff is gorgeous, but there really is so much more, including the areas outside the national parks.

On this road trip through the Canadian Rockies, we're going to visit some beautiful towns, some unique waterfalls, and spend time enjoying the many bodies of water in the rugged mountains of Alberta and British Columbia. As you plan your lodging along this road trip route, be open to staying in places that aren't in the middle of the action. This will save you a lot of money, and in some cases you'll actually enjoy the area even more than the more famous towns.

Start: Fly into Calgary, AB (YYC) and head right out of town. If you need to spend the night here because you're arriving late, that's fine. The drive for the first leg of this road trip is fairly short and easy. **Sleep in:** Calgary or Canmore

Day 1: No, we're not going into Banff National Park yet. Today is all about Canmore and exploring the foothills of the Rockies. Begin with a morning paddle on Barrier Lake outside Kananaskis. The turquoise mountain water is just the start of what you'll see on this road trip. From here, grab a picnic lunch and head to Grotto Canyon for a unique hike through the forest and narrow gorges, crossing all kinds of rocks to come face-to-face with petroglyphs and epic cliff walls. You may be tired after the hike, so make your way to downtown Canmore for an early dinner or a float on the Bow River. Don't miss the sun setting over the Rockies. **Sleep in:** Canmore

Day 2: Wake up early and head into Banff National Park. Because Moraine Lake and Lake Louise are so popular, you'll need to arrive *very* early if you'd like to see or hike around either of them. They truly are gorgeous and it's worth it, but if you don't get there *very* early you won't get a chance to see these famous lakes. After you're done at the lakes, head to Johnston Canyon to hike through the gorge with icy blue and green water churning below you, spilling falls over falls. End your day of exploring around the town of Banff making stops at the Vermillion Lakes and Bow Falls. Have dinner downtown. **Sleep in:** Canmore

Day 3: Drive west through Banff National Park to Kootenay National Park. This is a picnic day, so be sure to have lunch ready to roll with you. Being a lesser visited area, there are some rugged sights to see, starting with a stop at Marble Canyon. The nearby Paint Pots are fascinating and if you like, you can hike to them from Marble Canyon. Hop back in the car and drive a bit to Numa Falls. As you continue along the Kootenay River, you'll end your day at Radium Hot Springs. **Sleep in:** Radium Hot Springs

Day 4: Since you're here, you might as well begin the day with a soak in the healing waters of Radium Hot Springs. After that, head over to Sinclair Canyon for some easy hiking. Watch for bears in the Columbia National Wildlife Area as you drive north to Golden, and then stop to hike at Lower Bugaboo Falls. As you continue on, the braided river guiding you is a portion of the headwaters of the Columbia River, which ends at the Pacific Ocean between Washington and Oregon. Walk along the river in downtown Golden and enjoy local beer and music for dinner. **Sleep in:** Golden

Day 5: Golden is considered the Rocky Mountain Trench, so today head up out of the trench with your picnic and into Glacier National Park. Start with a simple hike at Quartz Creek to a gorgeous glacial lake. Take it up a notch with another hike, the Great Glacier Trail, located just west of the Illecillewaet Campground. This will take about three hours. For a relaxing experience in the old growth forest, head just a bit farther west to the Hemlock Grove Boardwalk. On your way back to Golden, stop at Bear Creek Falls for a short but beautiful stroll to a roaring waterfall. **Sleep in:** Golden

Day 6: Yoho National Park is up next. Drive to Takakkaw Falls for a breathtaking double waterfall, as well as a variety of beautiful trails along the river flowing from it. Working your way back toward Golden, the next stop is Emerald Lake, which looks like a fairy tale, including its lodge. Do the simple loop trail around the lake or rent a kayak or canoe to explore. Enjoy lunch here at the lake before heading to Hoodoo Creek. This is a slightly longer hike, but still doable if you've had an active morning. Finish exploring Yoho National Park with a gentle walk through the woods to Wapta Falls. By the end of the day, you'll be tired but will have loved every minute of Yoho. **Sleep in:** Golden

Day 7: This is an optional day. If you don't want to make the journey up to Jasper National Park, head back to Calgary or spend more time in Banff. If you choose to head north to Jasper National Park, leave early so you can still catch wildlife doing their morning routine along the Icefields Parkway. One day catching the big sights of Jasper will be enough but consider this day a preliminary research trip for your next visit.

Start with an easy stop at Athabasca Falls, where the Athabasca River plunges seventy-five feet. From there, continue north for a hike at Valley of the Five Lakes. The colors will astound you. This is as far north as we'll go, so get back in the car and make your way to Sunwapta Falls, which isn't as big as Athabasca Falls, but is just as beautiful as it crashes down a horseshoe gorge. End the day in Jasper with a walk on the Columbia Icefield Skywalk (which may be terrifying if you're afraid of heights). As you wrap up your day in Jasper, if there's time, make stops at the many natural points of interest along the way (such as waterfalls and viewpoints), or visit some of the sights in Banff National Park that you didn't get to on your first drive through it. **Sleep in:** Canmore

Depart: Fly home out of Calgary (YYC). If you would like to add on to this trip, you can head south from Calgary and visit Waterton Lakes National Park and then continue down into Montana to visit Glacier National Park. Really, this road trip through the Canadian Rockies can easily take you through a large portion of the United States' Rockies too. And it's all worth exploring!

THE VANCOUVER ISLAND LOOP

I feel so fortunate that I've gotten to spend so much time on Vancouver Island. Its communities, nature, and combination of cultures make it a wonderful destination to explore. It's very easy to get to the island from Seattle or Vancouver, and whether you want an outdoor experience or to just relax and take in the people, Vancouver Island won't disappoint.

Because Vancouver Island is a popular destination with many Pacific Northwest residents and beyond, consider this a very strong suggestion to be sure you have your hotel reservations in advance and that your travel plan isn't too ambitious. You'll want to stick with your initial plan as best as possible.

Start: Fly into Vancouver (YVR) or Seattle (SEA) and then catch the boat to Vancouver Island. From the US you can drive onto the MV Coho (Black Ball Ferry Line) in Port Angeles, or the Washington State Ferry from Anacortes. Both of these will deliver you to the Greater Victoria area of Vancouver Island. From Vancouver, you can take BC Ferries from either Tsawwassen or Horseshoe Bay to either Nanaimo or the Greater Victoria area. Ultimately, they all get you to a good starting point. **Sleep in:** Victoria

Day 1: Wake up and get ready for a city made for breakfast. Breakfast is the most popular meal in Victoria, so pick a spot early or plan to wait outside. The Victorian neighborhood surrounding Chinatown (Canada's oldest) is a hub of good food and unique shopping. As you stroll through  the city, watch for more than twenty totem poles throughout. Visit the Royal BC Museum for an incredible permanent exhibit of First Nations art and artifacts, then cross the street for a tour of the iconic Parliament Building. If weather permits, have dinner outside looking out across Inner Harbour. **Sleep in:** Victoria

Day 2: Today we're visiting farm country and enjoying some beautiful gardens. Head east to the Sidney area of Vancouver Island for a relaxing day, touring at your leisure. On the way to Sidney, watch for fields of sunflowers and farm stands. Once in town, stroll along the waterfront grabbing a bite in the marina before you head out on the water for either a whale watching or eco-cruise experience. When you're back on land, head to Brentwood Bay to visit the famous Butchart Gardens. If you're visiting over the holidays, go at night for the lighting displays. **Sleep in:** Victoria

Day 3: Making your way up the eastern coast of Vancouver Island, keep your eyes peeled for the many wineries and vineyards. Have a day to focus on culture, heading inland to Cowichan Valley, starting at the Kinsol Trestle for a short hike and then visiting Duncan and Maple Bay where you'll find galleries, indigenous art, and kayaking, and ending at Lake Cowichan for a late lunch. On your way to Nanaimo, you'll find more quiet towns and Cowichan River Provincial Park. Plenty of wineries between there and Nanaimo will give you the chance to take your time and travel slow up the island. **Sleep in:** Nanaimo

Day 4: After some breakfast in Nanaimo, begin the drive north stopping first at Rosewall Creek Provincial Park and Nymph Falls Nature Park before you arrive in Campbell River. Have some lunch on the river or harbor before you head to Elk Falls Provincial Park for some light hiking. The Elk Falls Viewing Platform is just a few minutes' walk and includes a pretty long suspension bridge. The Campbell River Canyon View Trail is an awesome loop that includes lots of opportunities for wildlife viewing and even some totem poles. When you're done, if you want one more park, it's about a half-hour drive to Strathcona Provincial Park where you'll find some more beautiful waterfalls and wildlife. **Sleep in:** Campbell River

Day 5: Get up early to do the short ferry ride across the inlet to Quadra Island. Here you can visit Cape Mudge Lighthouse and spend some time up at the Nuyumbalees Cultural Centre learning about the indigenous peoples of the island. Take the ferry back across to Campbell River and then grab a picnic lunch for the road. Set your sights for Tofino on the west coast of the island, stopping at Rosewall Creek (waterfalls) or MacMillan (old growth forest) Provincial Parks along the way. Watch the sunset on the Pacific and have a beautiful meal in either Ucluelet or Tofino. **Sleep in:** Ucluelet or Tofino

Day 6: This part of Vancouver Island, Ucluelet/Tofino, is rarely visited but is gorgeous, with beautiful lodges and beaches. Known for whales frequenting the surrounding waters, keep an eye out for all types of marine life. Totem poles are a common sight both in Tofino and Ucluelet, and watch for indigenous art in galleries as well. In Ucluelet, visit Pacific Rim National Park via the beaches or the Rainforest Trail. Also, the Wild Pacific Trail is a great way to take in the nature of the area including the Amphitrite Point Lighthouse. Even this far out, you'll find breweries and distilleries, so support the locals and enjoy the evening on the coast. **Sleep in:** Ucluelet or Tofino

Day 7 (optional): Enjoy the long but beautiful drive to Port Renfrew. The dense rain forest has minimal services after you get through Port Alberni, so be sure you have a full tank of gas and some good snacks. You can also go via Nanaimo and the Cowichan Valley to save a bit of time and make some more wine country stops. Once at Port Renfrew, enjoy the town, hike through the Avatar Grove of old growth trees, and visit Botanical Beach Provincial Park. Known for its one-of-a-kind tidepools, the park is a treat! **Sleep in:** Port Renfrew

Depart: Drive back to Victoria or Nanaimo, depending on which boat off Vancouver Island you're taking. You can also fly out of Victoria (YYJ) if you prefer, but direct flights to most cities are very few and very expensive. If you want to keep on road-tripping, enjoy the Olympic Peninsula of Washington or head over to Vancouver and explore up the Sunshine Coast or to Whistler.

British Columbia is beautiful from every angle, so take your time and enjoy exploring!

THREE EASY AND SAFE
MEXICAN ROAD TRIPS

I'm often asked about road trips through Mexico and what my top recommendations are. While I haven't been to every region or driven every road, there are several Mexican road trips that I've done and loved. And yes, they've been easy and beautiful, even if the roads got a bit bumpy from time to time.

Before traveling to Mexico to do a road trip, there are a few things to take care of, most notably making sure that you've got the proper documentation for driving in Mexico. You'll need a passport and valid driver's license, and you'll also want to confirm your insurance coverage, both auto and medical.

Upon renting a car in Mexico, you're always presented with the option of purchasing additional Mexican insurance. Be sure to research in advance which additional coverage you might purchase in person. You'll most likely want to sign up for additional insurance, but you typically don't need the highest level suggested, sometimes forcefully, at the rental agency. Be prepared with knowledge.

When you hit the highway in Mexico, you'll find that the main roads are typically well maintained, although not always well lit. It's when you start to go off the beaten path a bit that roads can be a bit iffy. Do a little research before you head out, asking your hotel or wherever you're having breakfast what the road is like or if there are any recommendations for your trip.

Confidently drive off into the sunset and have a wonderful time exploring Mexico!

MAGIC OF THE YUCATÁN PENINSULA

I will never not appreciate how colorful Mexico is. From trips around Baja California Sur to road-tripping on the Yucatán, there are always new places to enjoy. The colorful towns of the Yucatán are exceptionally cool and fun, and each is so different! This road trip theme: colorful towns, street art, and nature. And ruins.

The Yucatán Peninsula is known for destinations such as Cancún and Tulum, but there are many more towns to visit. Beyond the beaches, the Yucatán has some of the most breathtaking natural and historical sites. This Yucatán road trip plan covers an ideal mix of all these things.

As you follow this road trip itinerary, or if you just use this as a jumping-off point, remember that you can always come back to the beach. It's very easy to include the beach within every day of travel, so unless there is a must-visit beach, this itinerary will not call out beach time. Feel free to just add it where you want it.

Another thing to note: While some of these activities are free or a part of the Mexican national park system, many natural wonders are actually located on private property, so you should expect to pay entrance fees, which can vary greatly. Cenotes, which are caves and sinkholes open to the surface, are phenomenal swimming spots and most are located on private property, so they have a fee.

So much to do, see, and discover!

Start: Fly direct to Cancún (CUN) from nearly any major airport in the US. From Canada, there are direct flights from both Toronto and Montréal (subject to change). Once you arrive, pick up your rental car and head to your hotel. You might as well get in a walk on the beach today, even if you arrive late. **Sleep in:** Cancún

Day 1: Wake up and take a walk on the beach, because you should start your day this way whenever possible. After breakfast, visit the Zona Arqueológica El Rey to explore the ruins directly in Cancún. Head south next to visit Puerto Morelos and walk the Malecón (waterfront walkway), jumping into the Caribbean if you need. Grab some lunch and then drive inland to Cenotes Siete Bocas. This small cenote zone includes a bit of cliff jumping and swimming underground through connected cave openings. End the day in Playa del Carmen where the nightlife and food will pleasantly surprise you. **Sleep in:** Playa del Carmen

Day 2: After finding some breakfast in Playa del Carmen, hop in the car and head south to Cenote Azul. This particular cenote is quite beautiful with colorful water and rocks to jump off. When you've had your fill of the freshwater, head to Akumal, where you can swim at Playa Akumal, aka Turtle Beach. Follow the guidelines and grab your snorkel as you swim out just far enough to watch green sea turtles eating and sleeping below you. Sit outside on a patio for lunch and then pop over to Cenote Yal-Ku, which actually connects out to the salt water. For one more, very different cenote experience, visit Cenotes Dos Ojos. While you may not want to join the scuba divers, you'll be amazed by the stalactites and stalagmites in these caves. **Sleep in:** Tulum

Day 3: Time to take a break from cenotes (if you want) and visit ruins. Begin your day at the archaeological ruins at Tulum. You can walk or bike to the main ruins area and then explore on your own or do a tour. Set directly over the Caribbean, the views are remarkable. When you're ready, jump on the road and head south to the Muyil ruins and the Sian Ka'an Biosphere Reserve. As a bonus, visit the Laguna de Kaan Luum as well. You'll be blown away by all the beauty today. Head back to Tulum to find dinner and refresh for tomorrow. **Sleep in:** Tulum

Day 4: Leave Tulum and travel west to the jungles of Cobá. Yes, we've got another set of ruins on the schedule. The Cobá Archaeological Park is very different in that it's *in* the jungle. Rent a bike or hire a bicitaxi to get to the great pyramid and enjoy the jungle atmosphere. If the park managers allow you to while you're there, climb the great pyramid and look across the treetops to see more pyramids that haven't been uncovered yet. Drive to the city of Valladolid next. The colorful buildings and promenade are a different side of Mexico not yet seen on this trip around the Yucatán. And with Volkswagen Beetles everywhere, it's really a fun town. To top it off, there's an enormous cenote, Zaci, in the middle of town. It's a *huge* open-face cave you can swim in. **Sleep in:** Valladolid

Day 5: Wake up and visit Chichén Itzá if you want to see more ruins, but if you have had enough, head straight to the city of Mérida. Here you will find more colorful streets, such as the Paseo de Montejo or the Parque Centenario. The Museum of Anthropology and History here is fascinating, and there are countless churches and cathedrals to visit. It's a major city with everything you would expect from a metropolitan area (even a water park). And if you want to see even more ruins, there are some in town, and in Izamal, the next town we will visit. **Sleep in:** Mérida or Izamal

Day 6: Wake up and head to Izamal (or wake up *in* Izamal). Often called the Yellow City, Izamal is a small town, smaller than Valladolid, and is quiet, beautiful, and the perfect place for breakfast and some morning exploring. Visit the convent and cathedral of San Antonio de Padua, explore some ruins in town, and then head to the north reaches of the Yucatán to Río Lagartos (also known as Las Coloradas) and the Parque Natural Ría Lagartos. Here you'll find pink lakes (used for evaporating salt out of water) and migrant flamingo populations. It's incredible. **Sleep in:** Río Lagartos, Las Colorados, or El Cuyo

Day 7: Make an early stop as you head back to Cancún at Cenote Kikil (if coming from Río Lagartos), which is another huge sinkhole cave. It's remarkable. When you arrive back in Cancún, spend the rest of your day on the beach at Playa Tortuga or Playa Langosta. Enjoy your last night in Mexico. **Sleep in:** Cancún

Depart: Fly back out of Cancún (CUN). If you feel you need less time traveling and more time relaxing, return your rental car and book a shuttle bus to spend a few days up on Isla Holbox. There are no cars on the small island and between the sunsets and the bioluminescence in the bay, you'll enjoy every moment. Another potential add-on is a few days on Isla Mujeres or even Cozumel. The possibilities around the Yucatán Peninsula are endless.

BAJA CALIFORNIA SUR ROAD TRIP

A road trip through Baja California Sur is one of my favorite vacations. It's perfect to do with kids and is even great solo. For this road trip itinerary, you have the option to make it affordable or go five-star the whole way.

Whether you're into sport fishing and fine dining, or if you want to hike to desert waterfalls and swim with sea lions, Baja California Sur is the place for you. There's a fair mix of history and nature as you complete your road trip. Colorful towns and pristine beaches make this one of the most beautiful and unforgettable trips around.

While you most likely won't have to go through military checkpoints like you find traveling through other parts of Mexico, it's a possibility. Be sure that you have tourist cards for everyone doing the road trip with you, and make sure your passports are safely packed.

Have a great trip, and if you're flexible and are having a great time, add on the optional days up to Loreto (at end of itinerary). You'll be so glad you did!

Start: Fly into San José del Cabo (SJD) direct from most major US airports. The airport is a fair distance from Cabo San Lucas (which is where most visitors head), but you can start your Baja California Sur road trip right near the airport in San José for a more mellow beginning (and you won't have to start your vacation with an hour's drive). **Sleep in:** San José del Cabo

Day 1: Start your day in old town San José, enjoying a wonderful outdoor breakfast. Wander the streets a bit for some shopping and visit the historic mission cathedral and grounds. Enjoy a nice lunch and then head to the estuary for a stroll before venturing to Buzzards Beach on the East Cape. You can also do a beach directly in town, but East Cape has some fascinating tide pools. **Sleep in:** San José del Cabo

Day 2: Either book a tour or take yourself up to Cabo Pulmo National Park. Once there, go with a guide to snorkel in Mermaids Lagoon, check out the reef, and watch for iguanas on the beach. The national park isn't as developed as American or Canadian parks are, but it's just as pristine and gorgeous. If you're driving yourself, return home via East Cape Road (a bit rough due to its remote location) and stop for a swim. After, grab dinner when you return to San José. Alternate route option is to take the main highway and stop in Caduaño on the way back. **Sleep in:** San José del Cabo

Day 3: Heading westward, change your home base to Cabo San Lucas. On the way, stop at Playa Chileno or Playa Santa Maria to lay on the beach, or for some really good snorkeling if it's a calm day. Once in Cabo, explore downtown, leaving the exploration of the marina until dinnertime. There are wonderful restaurants and artisan shops two to five blocks off the main road. Dinner is when you want to be in the marina, as the atmosphere is fun and the food choices fantastic. **Sleep in:** Cabo San Lucas

Day 4: After sitting down to eat breakfast burritos (or take them to go), head to the playa publica, also known as the Cannery Beach or Playa Empacadora. The sand is great, there are always street food vendors at the entrance with great options, and the snorkeling is the best in all of Cabo San Lucas. In the afternoon, go for a sail or snorkeling cruise to check out El Arco and watch for mobula rays jumping out of the water. An alternate plan for this day could be going on a guided dive trip out to Gordo Banks to swim with sharks, or for a less serious, less skilled adventure, go on a booze cruise (Cabo is known for them). **Sleep in:** Cabo San Lucas

Day 5: Head north out of Cabo San Lucas to Todos Santos. On the way, stop at either Secret Rocks Beach or Playa Pacifica for a swim. Note that the currents and waves on the Pacific side can be quite strong. Be smart and safe as you swim. Head north to Playa Cerritos for lunch and more beach time. When you're ready, drive into Todos Santos, *un Pueblo Magico*. This is where the Hotel California and the Mission (from the famed Eagles song) is located. Wander the streets, spotting the small carved saints above all the doorways. Enjoy dinner outside. **Sleep in:** Todos Santos

Day 6: Wake up in Todos Santos and have a relaxing breakfast before visiting the Centro Cultural and some of the many galleries and artisan shops. Make your way back over to the beach at Punta Lobos. This sheltered beach is beautiful and the perfect end to the Pacific side of the Baja California Sur road trip. After just an hour's drive, you will arrive in La Paz. When you arrive, walk the Malecón, take a dip in the bay, and have a great lunch at one of the many patio restaurants. In the late afternoon, head to Playa Balandra to relax and fall in love with the Sea of Cortez. Get a good night's sleep because tomorrow will be fun! **Sleep in:** La Paz

Day 6: Get up early to go on a snorkeling or diving expedition to see the whale sharks. Watch for dolphins, sea lions, a variety of whales, and colorful fish. If you choose to not do a full-day excursion, spend more time walking through the main old town area of La Paz. If you haven't yet been, visit the cathedral before having one last wonderful dinner in this beautiful town. **Sleep in:** La Paz

Bonus Plan: From La Paz, drive up to Loreto. A very different experience than San José or La Paz, Loreto is also full of history and is surrounded by incredible  beauty, both on the coast and inland. Loreto has several old missions close by, of which there aren't many more left on the Baja, as you head northward. Spend two or three days here and be sure to get out onto the water to swim with whale sharks. While you don't get the gray whale encounters in the Sea of Cortez that you get on the Pacific side, you can still venture out and watch for sperm whales, minke whales, fin whales, and more. The natural beauty of the area is amazing!

Day 7: Drive back to San José del Cabo today. Make it a fun drive, though, stopping to hike at a waterfall in Sierra de la Laguna. Also make sure to visit the towns of El Triunfo and Santiago, where colorful churches make for ideal stops (for lunch and walking around). End your day back in San José del Cabo. **Sleep in:** San José del Cabo

Depart: Fly out of San José del Cabo (SJD) or take the ferry over to Mazatlán to continue your journey through Mexico.

EXPLORING NORTHERN BAJA

Doing a road trip through Northern Baja California, Mexico, is a really fun and interesting option for either family travel or adventurous adults. A drive through Northern Baja is all about the rugged coast and beautiful valleys, and if you continue south, a Baja California Sur road trip gives you picturesque towns and amazing snorkeling experiences.

This road trip plan takes you from Tijuana to Bahía de los Ángeles. It includes wine country, lots of great food, beach time, and whale watching. A less touristy experience than Baja California Sur, you'll need to speak and understand Spanish better than you might expect. English isn't widely spoken, so exercise your language skills and patience as you explore.

Much of Baja California is undeveloped or sparsely so. With that, there aren't a ton of major sights and famous towns, but you get the freedom of finding quiet beaches and very small restaurants or roadside kitchens for meals. You'll love it.

Driving in the rural areas of Baja California, you can expect to come across military checkpoints from time to time. Be sure you have your passports and that you've registered with a tourist card once you've crossed the border into Mexico. If you flew in, you already have filled out the form and should have the tourist card on your person at all times.

Start: Fly into Tijuana (TIJ) or San Diego (SAN) to begin. Tijuana is a huge city, so if you want to spend a day exploring, it's definitely worth taking the time! Otherwise, head south to be ready to start the Baja California road trip first thing in the morning. For a more scenic yet slower drive, head west to Mexico Federal Highway 1D and make stops along the way at the many viewpoints and beaches. **Sleep in:** Rosarito

Day 1: Start your Baja road trip by walking on the beach. This is always a good idea, particularly since this itinerary has a fair amount of time inland. After the beach, explore the town a bit, including tequila tasting and looking for the perfect tin-framed mirror to bring home. Head south along the coast, stopping in Puerto Nuevo for lunch and more beach time. End your drive in Ensenada, a large town with a peaceful vibe. Dinner just off the Malecón finishes the day. **Sleep in:** Ensenada

Day 2: Walk through downtown to find breakfast before visiting the Riviera de Ensenada and Museo Histórico Regional. Take a peek inside the gorgeous cathedral and then have a torta for lunch. If you like, there's wine tasting locally as well, as the Valle de Guadalupe wine region isn't too far away. When you're ready, head south, visiting La Bufadora (the blowhole) and supporting the locals selling their wares. Continue on your journey toward Santo Tomás where you'll head west to the coast. The road may be a bit rough, so be prepared. Stop at any beach or rocky point that suits you along the way, ending your day in a small town on the Pacific. **Sleep in:** Erendira

Day 3: Relax at the beach or head out fishing with a local guide. By late morning, you should be on the road again heading toward Rancho los Pinos. Here you'll have time to relax, snorkel, fish, and just enjoy the small-town Mexican culture. **Sleep in:** Rancho los Pinos

Day 4: Today the drive takes you across the desert and mountains of Baja California. There is a lot of driving to do (5.5 hours), but you can easily break it up with stops to enjoy the mountains. This includes a few roadside hikes. Safety first: Be sure you're well stocked with water and snacks, and that you get gas before heading away from the beach. Fill up in El Rosario and then again in San Antonio de las Minas. There are many small cafés and food stands along the drive, so getting lunch to go is easy. When you arrive in Bahía de los Ángeles, you can relax. You'll be here for a few days. **Sleep in:** Bahía de los Ángeles

Day 5: Explore the coves and beaches of Bahía de los Ángeles. If you like, book a boat trip over to any of the small islands just offshore, or to Punta El Pescador. If the season is right, opportunities for swimming with whale sharks and sea lions are available. The Sea of Cortez is incredible for snorkeling and diving, so enjoy! **Sleep in:** Bahía de los Ángeles

Day 6: Another day to enjoy the Sea of Cortez! Make lots of stops along the way as you head north to San Felipe. Stop for lunch and beach time in Puertecitos. This is a very rural area with a small population, so take advantage of the gas stations and food options as they come up. When you arrive in San Felipe, walk the Malecón and enjoy the town. There are several nice hotels to choose from and plenty of dining. **Sleep in:** San Felipe

Day 7: You have two choices for today. You can either spend one more day in San Felipe playing in the Sea of Cortez and then drive all the way back to Tijuana tomorrow, or you can head to Valle de Guadalupe to have a day touring Baja California wine country. With more than twenty wineries, vineyards, and tasting rooms, you can have a very different sort of wine tasting experience than you might have in Temecula or Napa. **Sleep in:** Guadalupe or Ensenada

Depart: Drive back to either Tijuana or San Diego to round out your Baja California road trip. You could also head east to explore the eastern side of the Sea of Cortez, including Golfo de Santa Clara and Puerto Peñasco. Whichever way you go, you'll no doubt want to return to Baja California for another road trip soon!

AFTERWORD

SHARING MY KNOWLEDGE of and experiences in travel, and specifically of road trips, is very special to me. Both as a kid and now as an adult with my own kids, road trips have been at the core of many of our most special family memories. Thinking back, even before kids, my favorite memories with my husband are all road trip related.

The world has changed so much in the twenty-first century, particularly in what we consider as accessible or safe travel. As society evolves and more and more people learn about the world beyond their backyard, road trips are only going to continue to grow in popularity. It's exciting to consider the possibilities that lie on the road ahead.

Cost and safety in all areas of travel are at the forefront of many people's minds. That's why road trips are such a fantastic option:

- Complete control over activities and interactions
- You can manage your accommodations in many different ways
- Road trips allow for a range of budgets
- Learning opportunities and beautiful sights are endless

As you start to plan your own road trips, consider the many choices you can make to create incredible experiences. I think, looking back through the chapters of *The Road Trip Survival Guide*, there are great possibilities. Whether you're heading out on your own to photograph rural mountain towns, or if it's a family trip to reconnect, putting thought and preparation into a trip will make a world of difference.

THE FUTURE OF TRAVEL

Moving forward, the future of travel is going to look very different from what most adults grew up with. Yes, flying and checking into a five-star, all-inclusive resort will still be an option that many will take, but as we've seen health and politics take a front seat in our lives, simpler travel that is thoughtful and considerate of the world around us will become more prevalent.

Being a travel writer, I have access to the deep, personal thoughts of many others who work in the industry: hospitality, destinations, marketing, other writers, etc. The common belief is that travel with a positive impact is going to become the primary choice for many. Travel that puts money back into the communities people visit versus back into corporate mega-machines may become the norm, and I certainly hope so. Travelers of all sorts are understanding more and more how their actions impact the natural world, so eco-tourism and low-impact travel methods may grow exponentially in the coming years.

Considering how things have changed since I started planning my own travel adventures in comparison to today when I plan for our whole family, I can see how I've morphed my methods. Whereas I used to just travel based on budget and the biggest bang for my buck, now I think about the quality of experience and ultimately where my dollars will go. I think about how our journeys leave a mark on the places we visit, so we are more careful to travel gently, minimize waste, and leave nature exactly as we found it.

That's what I hope for with everyone as travel continues to change. As you and those you travel with make big plans, be actively seeking out the experiences that give back or that positively affect the area you're in. Make road trip travel a learning adventure, not just about history, but about the people you meet and what makes them unique. Be inspired by visits to national parks to make changes in your daily life that benefit preservation and conservation of our natural wonders and resources.

Enjoy hitting the road, seeing the world with fresh eyes, and creating new memories with every mile. Happy traveling!

ACKNOWLEDGMENTS

THANK YOU TO my travel friends and peers, who've suffered through road trips with me and encouraged me when the world came to a halt:

To Kelly, for helping me appreciate the privilege I have; to Karilyn, for joining me on the journeys; and to Samantha, for showing me the value of sharing meaningful experiences.

To Barbara, for showing us the magic of Florida and helping us find a place to land. To Chrisie, for trusting me to tell the stories that need to be told. To Angie, for showing me how to be nimble and move with the changing times (and laugh about it).

And thank you to the many destinations we've worked with over the years that have helped us dig into the heart of the places we visit.

All of these people and places have been invaluable, personally and professionally, through the years. Thank you for being incredible and sharing your world with me.

NOTES

CHAPTER 1: PLANNING

1. "Gatekeeping: Definition of Gatekeeping by *Oxford Dictionary* on Lexico.com Also Meaning of Gatekeeping," Lexico | English (Lexico Dictionaries, n.d.), https://www.lexico.com/en/definition/gatekeeping.
2. "Climate Change: Should You Fly, Drive or Take the Train?" BBC News, August 23, 2019, https://www.bbc.com/news/science-environment-49349566.

CHAPTER 3: ROAD TRIP FOOD

1. "The Menorcans," National Parks Service, US Department of the Interior, 2015, https://www.nps.gov/foma/learn/historyculture/menorcans.htm.

CHAPTER 4: SAFETY

1. "Emergency: Definition, Pictures, Pronunciation and Usage Notes: Oxford Advanced American Dictionary at OxfordLearnersDictionaries.com," *Oxford Advanced Learner's Dictionary* at OxfordLearnersDictionaries.com, https://www.oxfordlearnersdictionaries.com/us/definition/american_english/emergency.

INDEX

ABOUT THE AUTHOR

Rob Taylor is the founder and lead journalist for *2TravelDads*, the original LGBT family travel blog. Focusing on travel as a form of education, *2TravelDads* showcases brands and destinations that are ideal for families of all kinds. Partnering with brands such as IHG, Universal, VISIT FLORIDA, Amtrak, and more, *2TravelDads* creates content for its own channels as well as branded media for partners. He lives in Florida with his husband and two sons.